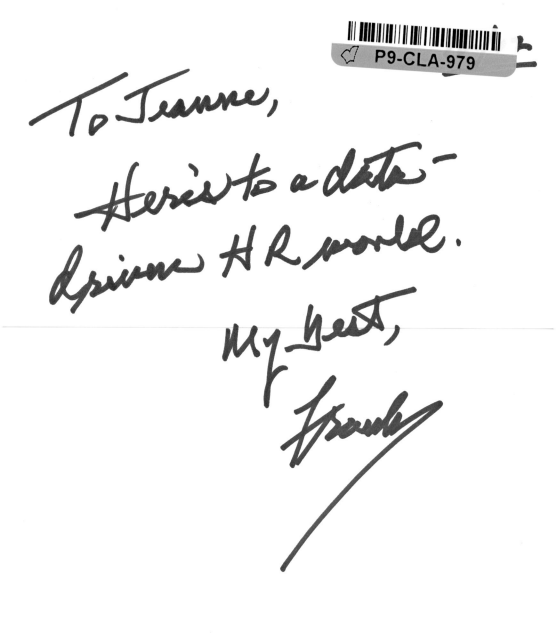

To Jeanne,

Here's to a data-driven HR world.

My Best,

Frank

OPTIMIZE HUMAN CAPITAL INVESTMENTS

INVESTMENTS

Make the "Hard" Business Case

Frank J. DiBernardino

Founder And Managing Principal
Vienna Human Capital Advisors, LLC

First published by Dog Ear Publishing
4010 W. 86th Street, Ste H
Indianapolis, IN 46268
www.dogearpublishing.net

ISBN: 978-1-4575-1466-1

This paper is printed in the United States of America

CONTENTS

PREFACE

This book is about context in the field of human capital analytics. It offers a comprehensive, cohesive, and cascading method for a Chief Human Resource Officer (CHRO) to analyze the financial performance of the organization's investments in human capital. Moreover, it lays out a process to convert hard results into human capital strategy that will lead to continuous improvement in business results. But first some background.

Shortly after launching Vienna Human Capital Advisors in 2004, my partner and I met with the CEO of a pharmaceutical company who asked an innocent enough question: *"What is the best way to measure HR's performance?"* She went on to say that her company invests a lot of money in people and programs, and HR seems to have an endless appetite for more of the company's limited financial resources. But how can she be assured those precious financial resources are producing bottom-line results? A fair question, and a timely one indeed.

We thought surely there must be an established approach we could use to answer her questions, so we embarked on an HR research project. To our surprise, we couldn't find any credible approach that could answer her questions. Sure, there had been a lot written on the topic, but nothing that we could find that would pass a CFO sniff test. Having done lots and lots of benefits consulting, I learned that numbers needed to be hard if they were going to get through Finance review. And if Finance didn't sign off on the numbers, the CEO wouldn't either.

If the HR world didn't have hard numbers to answer these questions, where did one turn? For Vienna, we had the good fortune, serendipitous as it was, to meet a Wharton MBA at an Association for Corporate Growth (ACG) event. This gentleman had been a CFO and private equity fund executive during his career. He also happened to have an aeronautical engineering degree from UVA, so he was a rocket scientist, as well. Suffice it to say, he is a pretty smart chap. He subsequently introduced us to the DuPont formula. This formula combines three universally accepted financial methods to calculate a value. The component formulas are for ROI, productivity and financial leverage. You'll find these formulas in any finance textbook. Any financial executive worth his or her salt knows them.

Even this dull blade could conclude that if we could develop corollaries to these universally accepted formulas that isolated and measured the human capital investment financial performance, the finance folks would salute the results.

After lots of trial and error with constructive feedback from several accomplished finance and HR executives we developed formulas that measure the productivity, ROI, and liquidity of the human capital investment. It wasn't rocket science, but it was a long, complex, enlightening, and worthwhile journey!

Having hard numbers is one thing, knowing what to do with them is quite another. The next challenge was to show how to dissect the numbers to understand what was driving the results and identify the changes in human capital strategy that will improve business performance.

This book pulls it all together. We describe how to calculate the human capital ROI, productivity that drives the ROI, and liquidity that protects the ROI. We also explain why the formulas are constructed as they are.

We lay out a comprehensive method to analyze the results and identify the modifications in human capital strategy that will improve business performance. And we show how to calculate the impact on shareholder value of the improvement in human capital ROI.

This is not an academic approach, but a very practical, hands-on model that has been field tested. Using the methods presented in this book will enable the CHRO to effectively respond to the CEO challenge to demonstrate value and make the necessary business case for the investments in human capital to continuously improve business performance.

ACKNOWLEDGEMENTS

This book never would have been possible without the generous support of a number of people. These individuals have been very kind and very willing to provide candid and constructive feedback on the material included herein.

Michael McClure, Adrianne Miller, and Frank Zirnkilton deserve special mention. Frank provided the inspiration for the Vienna Human Capital Index™ formulas by introducing us to the DuPont Formula.

Michael, a friend and former client, is the coinventor of the Vienna Index™ formulas. When we had developed a crude version of the formulas, I reached out to Michael. While we had the proper elements for the formulas, Michael applied the proper algebra. He has been with me every step of the way, ever helpful and more patient with me than I had any right to expect. Over countless lunches at Ventura's or Ott's we have discussed every nuance of the formulas and the analytic methods.

Adrianne Miller, a Vienna Human Capital Advisors colleague and former Chief Human Resource Officer (CHRO), has been most helpful in developing the Vienna Index software and vetting every aspect of the formulas and analytic approach. Having been a highly accomplished CHRO, Adrianne was most generous with her wise counsel on how to position the Index. Adrianne has been forever patient in helping me get to the proper conclusion she reached long before on an issue I was struggling to get through.

Others have been generous with their advice throughout this process including Jim Geier, my original Vienna partner; Pat Lawrence, a former Vienna colleague; several financial folks including Steve Blodgett, an investment banker, Jonathan Alt, a private equity executive, and Mike Dinkins, former CFO of Hilb, Rogal and Hobbs; our patent attorneys Greg Bernabeo of Saul Ewing, Josh Slavitt of Pepper Hamilton, and Richard Jaffe of Duane Morris. Jane McLaughlin and Carla Russo of LifeCycle Software and Skip Shuda from Dream and a Team helped with the technology side. Our accountant, Craig Springer, was most generous with his time and constructive feedback throughout this process.

Bill Delorbe and Mary Beth Yannessa deserve special mention. Bill put us on the path of precisely articulating the elements of the human capital investment (employee costs, costs in support of employees, and costs in lieu of employees). This was a major breakthrough in the development of the concept. Mary Beth Yannessa, CEO of Tridon Industries, our alpha client, who challenged us to put the Vienna Human Capital Index results in a business context.

Francine Carb and Jen Allen have helped us write or edit most of what we have published on the topic. The members of the Greater Philadelphia Senior Executive Group (GPSEG), Entrepreneur's Circle subgroup have been most helpful in providing keen advice on business issues I struggled with. And Steve Smolinsky of Benari, Ltd convinced me I should write this book. And thank you Anne Dubuisson Anderson for your masterful work in editing every word in this book, and bringing clarity and cohesion to my disorganized and sometimes incomplete thoughts.

Finally, a special mention is reserved for Jim Sowers, of Wipro Consultants, and Ray Slabaugh, Dave Morgan, and Joe Birriel formerly of Hilb, Rogal & Hobbs (HRH). Jim while at Buck Consultants, Ray, Dave, and Joe, while at HRH, all invested in the development of the Vienna Index approach and software by conducting and underwriting the cost of pilot projects. Without their financial resources, the Vienna Human Capital Index would today be an undeveloped idea.

CHAPTER 1

MEASURING HUMAN CAPITAL INVESTMENT PERFORMANCE

"Measurement systems create the basis for effective management."

– Fredrick Reichheld, Bain & Company

Companies invest in human capital (people and HR programs) to drive revenue, profits, and shareholder value. Moreover, as the chart below shows, companies invest far more in human capital than financial capital.

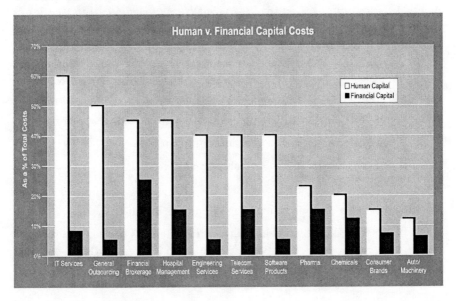

Source: Boston Consulting Group

Despite investing more in human capital, companies do not normally measure the financial performance of the human capital investment. On the other hand, the processes for measuring the performance of financial capital are well established and include such measures as ROI (profit/assets), productivity (revenue/assets), return on equity (profit/shareholder equity), margin (profits/revenue) and many other advanced concepts such as economic value added (EVA), internal rate of return (IRR) and total shareholder return (TSR). Nearly every nuance of measuring the performance of financial capital is well documented and used by various constituents for their purposes.

Yet, in today's economy, human capital is the foundation of value creation. The people investment drives the profits and value of the business. While financial capital (cash) is the lifeblood of a business, it is people that deploy the cash and drive business performance. Various studies show that 85% of a corporation's value is based on intangible assets (Becker, Huselid, and Ulrich, 2001). While other forms of capital, including material, equipment, tools, and technology, only represent inert potentialities, it is the human capital that converts this potential and energizes the creation of organization wealth.

WHY MEASURE THE HUMAN CAPITAL INVESTMENT

Several distinguished authors in the human capital space have offered numerous reasons why companies should measure human capital investments. As Dr. Jac Fitz-enz observed in *The ROI of Human Capital:* "Information is the key to performance management. Without it, we have no supporting facts and no directional signals." Dr. John Sullivan offered a similar comment in *HR Metrics... The World-Class Way* when he wrote: "Without numbers, it's just an opinion." In *The New HR Analytics*, Jac Fitz-enz observes the following reasons for human capital analysis and measurement:

1. If you don't *measure* it, you don't know what is actually happening
2. If you don't *understand* it, you can't control it, and
3. If you can't *control* it, you can't improve it

Additional benefits of using human capital metrics include:

1. Eliminating confusion about what is important. What you measure and reward sends the clearest possible message to your employees about what is important.

2. Creating parameters for continuous improvement. Knowing what is expected focuses attention on what changes will drive improvements.

3. Demonstrating a results-oriented mentality. CEOs need to know HR is striving to improve business performance.

4. Modifying behavior. The use of metrics has proven to be a powerful tool in changing behavior because it steers any potential conflict away from opinions and personalities and toward the facts.

These are compelling reasons why it is vital that companies measure the performance of their investment in human capital. While human capital metrics are not an end in themselves, they must be calculated to make the most effective resource allocation decisions to optimize organization financial performance. Bottom line–HR can't legitimately claim its share of the firm's financial resources unless it can show how it contributes to the firm's financial success.

The challenge of isolating the human capital investment

The investments that companies make in people (pay, benefits, training and development, other support costs, and outsourcing) are shown as expenses on the Income Statement. Also, you will not find the people investment in the asset column of a Balance Sheet.

This thinking is a carryover from days gone by when labor was viewed only as a cost of manufacturing and the value of people in the enterprise was never taken into account. So, it is not surprising that existing measurement tools fail to adequately inform decisions on the strategic use of human capital. In business, people metrics pose a complex challenge because human capital investments are dispersed throughout the general ledger in ways that disguise their scope and inhibit their comprehensive management.

Need to add value

Conventional HR metrics are not meeting the needs of CEOs and boards. In the *Fast Company* magazine article "Why We Hate HR," Keith Hammonds, Deputy Editor of the magazine observed, "HR pursues efficiency instead of value…easy to do and easy to measure." HR managers invest more importance in activities than in outcomes. "You're only effective if you add value. That means you're not measured by what you do, but by what you deliver," according to Dave Ulrich. And as Dr. Jac offered in *The New Human Capital Analytics*,

"Basically, no one in the organization cares what is happening with the human resources function. All they want to know is what value HR is generating for the company." Note in all three of these quotes the authors emphasize the concept of value added.

In the Society for Human Resource Management (SHRM) "Strategic HR Management Survey Report," HR professionals identified their most prevalent barrier to making effective contributions in the workplace as "the inability to directly measure HR's impact on the bottom line" and a lack of "an established method for measuring the effectiveness of HR strategy through metrics and analytics." This notion is reinforced in the Bersin & Associates Research Report "The Top Best Practices for the High-Impact HR Organization," which concludes that the single biggest challenge of the HR function is measuring HR programs in financial terms. Thirty-five percent of 720 participating companies in the Bersin survey identified this as their biggest challenge. In addition, 26% reported that their second biggest challenge was delivering workforce metrics and analytics. However, as Jack Phillips of the ROI Institute noted, "We're still measuring efficiencies, volumes, activities…the same things we were measuring twenty-five years ago. We're not measuring effectiveness."

STAKEHOLDER NEEDS

The human capital analytics journey must begin with understanding the information needs of the stakeholders. The stakeholders include the CEO and board, other functional leaders (i.e., Chief Financial Officer, Chief Information Officer, Chief Marketing Officer), and the leaders of the business units. Other stakeholders include the HR staff, who need to measure the value and quality of service to their constituents and service providers.

The CEO and board want to know how well the investment in human capital is performing and the leading indicators that will impact future performance. Measuring and reporting on the ROI and productivity of the human capital investment, over time and against plan, helps the CEO and board, in a manner similar to financial performance measures, gauge the financial performance of the business as a whole. However, like any ROI or productivity measure, they are lagging indicators of success. This reporting naturally leads to questions about what is driving the performance level and what actions can be taken to continuously improve results.

Leading indicators, however, are those measures that suggest whether future performance will improve or deteriorate. Some of the metrics that fit into this category include: employee engagement, new hire quality, voluntary turnover, and succession pool coverage.

Business unit leaders needs are quite similar to those of the CEO and board. Is the human capital investment performing at an acceptable level? What do the leading indicators tell us? In addition, HR operation cycle times and costs are also important and relevant measures for the business unit leaders. For instance, how long does it take to fill open jobs? What is the cost per hire or recruiting cost ratio?

The authors of *Ultimate Performance* (Burkholder, Golas, and Shapiro) include a useful exercise to categorize metrics according to the audience to confirm you are using the right metric for the right audience. A simple categorization of HR metrics according to audience is as follows:

- **Managing Up.** Metrics that are meant to satisfy objectives that HR and executive teams have agreed will impact larger business objectives.

- **Managing Out.** Metrics that can also leverage change within the constituents that you serve.

- **Managing Down.** These metrics, likely the most frequently used within HR, optimize the performance of the HR operations. These metrics have interest to managers within HR and to those that are being measured, but have little interest outside of the HR organization.

In summary, understanding the needs of the various stakeholders should be the context in which any HR or human capital analytics process is organized. To do otherwise undercuts HR's credibility.

THE INADEQUACIES OF CURRENT APPROACHES

While useful in other strategic contexts, none of the traditional methods for evaluating business performance isolate the human capital investment and determine whether it is improving or eroding a company's economic value.

Standard financial metrics–such as return on invested capital (ROIC), return on assets (ROI), return on equity, and cash flow proxies such as free cash flow (FCF)- are simply too broad to isolate and measure human capital performance.

Business unit performance measures and functional measures (for Sales and Marketing, Operations, HR, etc.) have similar limitations. They are unable to isolate the economic impact of people, and they are too segmented to explain what is driving the performance of the organization as a whole.

Worse yet, some of the most common human capital metrics can actually mask an organizational performance issue. Take, for instance, the time-honored measures of "Per Full Time Equivalent" (per FTE) and "Salaries and Benefits as a Percentage of Revenue." Both are incomplete and misleading because neither considers the aggregate of all internal and external human capital costs. Even good per FTE numbers (FTE expense as a % of X) do not consider outsourcing costs.

Here is an example of how per FTE numbers can mislead. A client with 40+ business units throughout the United States used profit per FTE as a business performance measure for the operating units. However, the CFO observed that the profit per FTE amount did not universally correlate with business unit margin. After months of investigation to reconcile this anomaly, the CFO discovered that several of the units outsourced some of their support functions, such as IT. In fact, the CFO learned that some of the business unit leaders were outsourcing support functions for the express purpose of improving the profit per FTE because of the impact on the incentive compensation pool. This "financial engineering," while increasing the incentive compensation pool, was undermining the profits of the business and shareholder value. This ultimately led to the redesign of the incentive compensation program design.

Likewise, any metric that draws numbers from HR-specific data sources (HRIS) is limited in its uses and cannot demonstrate a credible link between human capital performance and overall business results. Data latency is another significant issue with HR data. Despite companies best efforts, nobody has effectively solved the latency problem.

This is why the first step toward the next generation of human capital analytic capabilities must define and isolate the entire human capital investment. Only then can you evaluate its financial performance in terms of ROI, productivity, and liquidity-common and useful financial measures of business vitality.

A Closer Look at Per Full-Time Equivalent Data

Several prominent organizations promote the use of per full-time equivalent measures as a method to monitor how well the people investment is performing. For instance, McKinsey & Company regards Profit per Employee as a pretty good proxy for the return on intangibles.(Cao, Jiang & Koller, 2006) The Corporate Leadership Council, in its report "The Metrics Standard: Establishing Standards for 200 Core Human Capital Measures," recommends the use of Operating Revenue per FTE as a broad measure of the productivity of the workforce (2005). And the Saratoga Institute also recommends the use of Profit per Regular FTE as a key metric to take a balanced approach to managing a workforce.

Per-employee or per-full-time equivalent (FTE) measures can be useful to determine efficiencies of the organization's HR operations. But when it comes to measuring effectiveness for business planning purposes, per-employee measures can be incomplete, misleading, and suspect in the C-suite. Here are the issues:

The definition of an employee is inconsistent. There is no universally accepted definition of a full time employee equivalent. This is no small issue. How do you define an FTE when today's workforce consists of part-time or contingent employees, temporary employees, and outsourced jobs, projects, and services? Attempts to do so are tortured at best. Even within the same organization, it is common for HR, Finance, and Operations to define FTE differently. As a result, per-FTE numbers are not reliable as a valid common denominator across business units, peer organizations, or industries.

Apples-to-apples comparisons are elusive. Companies want to establish a baseline and measure performance and progress over time, across business units and against peer organizations. But for the reasons cited above, per-employee numbers do not provide standardized, credible data for apples-to-apples comparisons.

Profit per Employee is not an ROI measure. By definition, any ROI calculation needs to define and isolate an investment amount in dollars or other currency. Nowhere in the Profit-per-Employee or per-FTE formula has the investment been identified. If a company outsources jobs or replaces employees with machinery, Profit-per-Employee statistics may improve even when the underlying profitability or value of the company declines.

Revenue per Employee is a flawed productivity measure. While Revenue, or some version of Revenue, is the proper numerator in a productivity equation, use of a per-employee or per-FTE number as the denominator is flawed for the reasons cited previously.

Per-employee measures are not credible with the CFO. To be useful in the C-suite or boardroom for business planning purposes, any metric must pass the CFO smell test. CFOs, by and large, do not trust per-employee measures for all the reasons mentioned above.

A final observation on the shortcomings of per-FTE measures can be found in the seminal book, *The Balance Scorecard*, by Robert Kaplan and David Norton. The authors observed the following about the Revenue per-Employee ratio, "Another way of increasing the revenue per-employee ratio through denominator decreases is to outsource functions. This enables the organization to support the same level of output (revenue) but with fewer internal employees."

Other Issues with traditional HR metrics

Here are some of the common problems with traditional HR metrics as noted in *HR Metrics: The World Class Way*:

1. Too many metrics
2. Focus on effort, not output
3. Focus on quantity, not quality
4. Failing to establish a comparison over time, across business units or against peers
5. Failing to identify a trend
6. Not being credible in the eyes of senior management

Perhaps most alarming is a finding reported in a Conference Board report "Strategic Human Capital Measures" that the HR metrics most often used are not the ones most respondents believe best predict outcomes (i.e., leading metrics). Some of this is driven by the lure of fancy technology which produces results, but unfortunately, not the ones that are needed. And this shortcoming puts HR at a distinct disadvantage as a strategic partner in the C-suite.

In summary, stakeholders have a compelling need to measure the financial performance of the human capital investment, and understand what factors are driving the results. Existing approaches are inadequate.

Chapters Two through Five will demonstrate a different approach that will satisfy the demands of stakeholders, help you effectively analyze the factors driving the financial performance, and identify the necessary changes to human capital strategy to continuously improve business performance.

CHAPTER 2

MEASURING THE ROI, PRODUCTIVITY AND LIQUIDITY OF THE HUMAN CAPITAL INVESTMENT

"You can't improve your organization's performance without measuring it."

– Dean R. Spitzer, PhD

Two types of investments drive business results: human capital and financial capital. As noted in Chapter One, while financial capital (cash) is the lifeblood of the business, it is human capital, the body through which the lifeblood flows, that deploys the cash, and ultimately determines whether the deployed cash increases or destroys the value of the business enterprise.

Because the human capital investment of most organizations is significantly large, as shown in the chart in Chapter One, failure to accurately measure and optimize the human capital investment financial performance translates into a lost opportunity cost. Consider this cost magnified in today's economy, where all industries are experiencing a shift toward a greater proportion of service, knowledge, and talent-driven revenues.

For HR to demonstrate the value it adds to an organization, the time has come for business intelligence models that can provide a clear line of sight between investments in people, the corporate bottom line, and shareholder value. This is why the first step toward the next generation of human capital analytics capabilities must define and isolate the entire human capital investment. Only then can one evaluate its financial performance in terms of ROI, productivity and liquidity–the common and useful financial measures of business vitality.

SEVEN GUIDING PRINCIPLES

Given the deficiencies of current HR metrics and traditional financial measures, outlined in Chapter One, we propose seven Guiding Principles for Human Capital Analytics that will effectively address these shortcomings. These include the need to:

1. Identify the organization's entire investment in human capital. This investment consists of employee costs, costs in support of employees, and costs in lieu of employees. We will describe each of these items in detail, later in this chapter.

2. Use standardized, auditable data sourced from the organization's financial system. The only system of record that can provide hard, credible data is the financial system. It has the most up-to-date record of transactions, which is regularly scrutinized by auditors.

3. Define and measure data consistently. Consistent data is a precursor to credibly measure progress over time and compare results among business units.

4. Provide measures that are few in number, supported by diagnostic layers of relevant detail. Too many metrics create analysis paralysis. This view is shared by several distinguished authors in the field of human capital analytics. To effectively assess the performance of any investment, it's vital to have only a few measures that can be easily dissected to determine what is driving the level of performance.

5. Answer important strategic questions about what drives business results. To what extent is human capital versus financial capital driving business performance?

6. Provide a credible and clear line of sight between human capital investments and business performance. Is the human capital investment adding to or destroying enterprise value?

7. Apply straightforward methods that are resistant to being "gamed." Accounting for the entire investment in human capital and measuring the value added of the investment minimizes opportunities for financial engineering.

Abiding by these principles, people metrics could finally meet the full range of executives' needs. They would inspire confidence by drawing numbers straight from the general ledger. Measures would accurately reflect every dollar a company spends on people, and they would be calculated and compared consistently over time. A small, simplified set of indicators would make human capital performance easy to observe and analyze. Data would identify the major drivers of business results, alert management to emerging problems, and facilitate diagnoses and solutions.

METHODS TO MEASURE ROI, PRODUCTIVITY AND LIQUIDITY

Let's return to the CEO that asked the question about measuring HR's performance. She went on to say it would be wonderful if there were two or three metrics that she, and the other executives, could monitor that tell the story of how well the investment in people is performing.

CEOs are evaluated by the continuous, measurable improvement of business results. So, HR's challenge will be to show a direct link between human capital strategy, or any proposed changes in strategy, and a continuous improvement in the bottom line.

Given the CEO's dual challenge and the high likelihood that other CEOs have similar concerns, the question became: Are there current HR measures that can credibly meet this need? While many authors and organizations have written on this topic, none have:

- Isolated the entire investment in human capital. Thus, it was not possible to measure the investment's financial performance.

- Used financial data only. Using any data source, other than financial, simply undermines the credibility of the results. If the measures (formulas and data) don't pass a CFO smell test, they are likely to be discounted by a CEO or board.

Financial Metric Corollaries

Due to a dearth of credible HR metrics to measure human capital ROI, productivity, and liquidity, we looked to the world of financial metrics and found the DuPont Formula. The formula combines three well established financial measures for margin, productivity and financial leverage to create a unique value. This formula was developed in the early 1900s, is well known and respected in the financial community, and has stood the test of time. Also, the underlying formulas for margin, productivity, and financial leverage can be found in any college-level finance textbook. The linkage of the margin and productivity formulas is that one drives the other, productivity drives margin.

The margin formula is Profit/Revenue, and the productivity formula is Revenue/Assets. Assets, as shown on the Balance Sheet, are the monies a business invests to generate revenue and profits. Margin is typically expressed as a percentage (i.e., 20%), while productivity is expressed in dollars (i.e., $1.50).

The third measure of the vitality of a business enterprise is liquidity. Does the company have enough cash to pay its current expenses? There are various ways to measure liquidity, including the Current Ratio and Acid Test. The current ratio is the ratio of Current Assets to Current Liabilities, while the acid test is the ratio of Current Assets, less Inventory, to Current Liabilities. The acid test is a more strenuous measure of liquidity. CEOs and boards understand the importance of liquidity and are familiar with these formulas.

Given the significance of margin, productivity, and liquidity to the vitality of a business, could corollaries be developed in the HR space that would measure the vitality of the human capital investment and answer the CEO's challenge to create a set of metrics that would begin to tell the story of the financial performance of the human capital investment? As you will see below, it is possible to have such measures, but first, as suggested above, we need to identify the entire investment in human capital.

Human Capital Investment

We've made numerous references to the human capital investment, but just what is the human capital investment? Just as it is necessary to define the financial investment to calculate a financial ROI or productivity value, so it is that an organization must identify its human capital investment to accurately measure its ROI and productivity values.

The human capital investment consists of three elements:

- Employee costs
- Costs in support of employees
- Costs in lieu of employees

Employee costs consist of wages, benefits, and payroll taxes. These items are easily identified in a general ledger.

Costs in support of employees are the variable or incremental costs a company incurs to support its employees. These costs fall into the following categories: real estate or housing, communications, training and development, supplies, information technology (IT), and transportation. While also a part of the general ledger, all of these costs are not obvious. The test is whether the cost primarily supports the business or the employees. For example, Starbucks is a huge consumer retailer with locations worldwide. Most of Starbucks retail locations are leased and exist for the purpose of selling its products. Its corporate office in Seattle, Washington, on the other hand, exists primarily for the purpose of housing its employees. Thus, in this example the corporate office would be considered a cost in support of employees, while the retail outlets are not human capital costs as they exist to support the business. Another example is a payroll system. The payroll system exists to support the payment of wages/compensation to employees. Without employees, there would be no payroll system. This same process of distinguishing human capital costs versus costs of doing business would also be done for the other expense categories listed above.

Costs in lieu of employees are costs associated with independent contractors and outsourcing. The test of whether the expense is a cost in lieu of employees is if the expense replaces an employee that otherwise would perform the service. These costs are also part of the chart of accounts, though not always obvious. For example, charges for legal services may all be lumped under one category in the chart of accounts. However, when the question is posed: What portion of the legal fees incurred must be performed by outside counsel? The answer is typically less than 100%. The difference is the portion of cost that is outsourced. This is also true for services provided by the accounting/auditing firm, a firm that provides IT services, outsourced HR services, or other services provided by external vendors.

Thus, the process of reviewing the general ledger will identify a company's total or entire investment in human capital, the first step in measuring the ROI and productivity of the investment. These amounts come from the chart of accounts so they are updated regularly, "closed" monthly or quarterly, and scrutinized, by auditors, frequently.

Here is an example for a company that shows how these amounts are shown in a worksheet.

THE INCOME STATEMENT DATA

RETAIL REGIONS				
CATEGORY	**Southeast**	**Mid-Atlantic**	**Northeast**	**Central**
REVENUE				
Standard Commission & Fees	$16,522,330	$14,029,400	$33,618,606	$12,520,660
Non-Standard Commission and Fees	$1,202,376	$581,578	$2,375,806	$23,137
TOTAL COMMISSIONS AND FEES	**$17,724,706**	**$14,610,978**	**$35,994,412**	**$12,543,798**
HUMAN CAPITAL COSTS				
Employee Costs (Pay, Benefits & Taxes)				
Salaries & Commissions				
Brokers Commissions	$23,442	$163,345	$645,041	$164,979
Executive Salaries	$609,838	$135,494	$1,107,349	$372,834
Office Salaries	$2,860,546	$2,389,084	$6,492,023	$2,012,878
Sales Salaries (Variable Compensation)	$2,009,946	$1,933,275	$4,890,436	$2,800,334
Sales Commissions (Variable Compensation)	$1,501,206	$1,387,568	$133,355	$269,847
Bonuses				
Executive Bonuses	$17,501	$0	$0	$350
Office Bonuses	$111,226	$191,783	$114,877	$81,606
Sales Bonuses	$309,312	$536,298	$661,517	$220,877
Other Compensation and Benefits				
Deferred Compensation	$0	$0	$46,892	$0
Payroll Taxes	$433,928	$376,279	$1,014,700	$335,367
Employee Insurance	$543,828	$377,711	$498,437	$458,994
Profit Sharing Plan	$170,792	$134,357	$297,177	$109,841
Other Employee Benefits	$19,057	$2,254	($67,139)	$7,126
Total Employee Costs	**$8,610,623**	**$7,627,448**	**$15,834,666**	**$6,835,031**
% of Revenue	**48.6%**	**52.2%**	**44.0%**	**54.5%**
HC Costs - In Support of Employees				
Facilities Exp. (less Equip Repairs & Equip Dep)	$843,259	$609,331	$1,535,405	$411,390
Equipment Repairs & Maintenance	$85,460	$9,117	$22,024	$30,151
Telephone Expenses	$159,891	$94,315	$303,531	$105,892
Travel	$146,049	$84,035	$458,795	$77,631
Automobile Expense	$132,248	$144,712	$209,765	$113,926
Meeting Exp	$28,007	$7,143	$45,980	$48,229
Licenses and Taxes	$45,782	$43,329	$70,824	$42,677
Education & Training	$51,935	$25,933	$30,605	$57,269
Corporate Overhead	$719,885	$566,575	$1,496,017	$548,256
Indirect Overhead	$111,533	$136,443	$331,041	$117,293
Total HC Costs - In Support of Employees	**$2,324,049**	**$1,720,931**	**$4,503,988**	**$1,552,714**
% of Revenue	**13.1%**	**11.8%**	**12.5%**	**12.4%**
HC Costs - In Lieu of Employees				
Brokers Commission	$1,716,581	$723,289	$1,438,295	$36,990
Employment Fees & Expenses	$72,270	$69,498	$53,821	$57,791
Data Processing Expenses	$186,568	$111,025	$214,632	$116,771
Professional Services (Outsourcing)	$574,878	$76,616	$230,185	$130,424
Total HC Costs - In Lieu of Employees	**$2,550,297**	**$980,428**	**$1,936,932**	**$341,976**
% of Revenue	**14.4%**	**6.7%**	**5.4%**	**2.7%**
Total Human Capital Costs	**$13,484,970**	**$10,328,807**	**$22,275,586**	**$8,729,721**
% of Revenue	**76.1%**	**70.7%**	**61.9%**	**69.6%**

Financial Capital Costs

As will be shown in the formulas below, financial capital costs are also reflected in the calculation of the ROI and productivity values; and because they are included in the formulas, they need to be explained. We will clarify the rationale for including financial capital costs in the formulas in the next section.

Financial capital costs consist of interest, depreciation, amortization, and cost of equity. Interest is the amount paid to lenders for money borrowed through bonds or notes. Depreciation is an amount charged as an expense for amortization of tangible assets. Amortization is an amount charged as an expense for the depreciation of intangible assets. Cost of equity is the expected return on shareholder equity. The CFO can answer the question on the expected return on equity.

Interest, depreciation and amortization are shown on the income statement, whereas shareholder equity is shown on the balance sheet.

Appendix One is a sample data definitions document showing what items from the general ledger and the balance sheet were included in the data set as well as those items excluded.

Value-Added Formulas

The formulas for calculating ROI and productivity, as shown in the next section, are so-called value-added formulas. A value-added formula measures the incremental value of an investment, after adjusting for cost factors contemplated in the outcome. To illustrate, in an ROI formula, to determine the value added, the cost factor contemplated in the outcome (profit) is "cost of capital." Likewise, for a productivity formula, the cost factor contemplated in the outcome (revenue) is raw material costs, if any.

Thus, in an ROI formula, every dollar of profit beyond the cost of capital is the value-added profit. Whereas, with productivity every dollar of revenue, beyond the cost of raw materials, if any, is the value-added revenue.

Here is a simple example to illustrate the ROI value-added concept. Assume a company borrows $1 million at 5% interest for 1 year to buy an asset that it will sell 1 year later at a price of $1,150,000. At the end of the year, the company does indeed sell the asset for $1,150,000. From these proceeds, the company must pay the bank $1,050,000 ($1 million return of the loan and $50,000 interest). In this example, the company had an incremental value of the investment of $100,000 after adjusting for the "cost of capital" of $50,000. So, in a value-added formula, the ROI is 10% (($150,000 - $50,000)/$1 million). In a traditional ROI formula, the ROI would have been 15% ($150,000/$1 million). Not reflecting the cost of capital in the traditional ROI formula distorts the net gain to the investor as illustrated in this example. Such would be the case if an organization attempted to measure the ROI of its human capital investment and did not reflect the cost of capital in its calculation of ROI.

Measuring Human Capital ROI

Applying the above concepts to measure the ROI of the human capital investment, the numerator of the equation is profit, less financial capital costs (FCC). As previously identified, financial capital costs consists of interest, depreciation, amortization, and cost of equity.

Profit is defined as EBITDA (earnings before interest, taxes, depreciation, and amortization). EBITDA is a credible, universal financial performance measure that works for all kinds of business enterprises–both privately-held and publicly-traded companies. EBITDA is a good metric to evaluate profitability and works well in all cases because it reflects profit irrespective of the financial capital structure (debt vs. equity) of the business, which can vary greatly by industry/organization.

$$\text{HC ROI} = \frac{\text{EBITDA} - \text{Financial Capital Costs}}{\text{Human Capital Investment}}$$

An interesting dimension of this approach to measuring the ROI of the human capital investment is the premise that human capital has added no incremental value to the enterprise unless it first generates enough profit to exceed the financial capital costs of the business. In fact, if financial capital costs aren't recovered, the value of the enterprise is being destroyed! In *What the CEO Wants You to Know*, Ram Charan emphasizes the importance of this distinction: "If the return on investment does not exceed the cost of capital, there will be real discontent among the investors because management is destroying shareholder wealth." The flip side to this premise is that every dollar of profit generated, beyond financial capital costs, is the exclusive result of the human capital investment. This observation adds great leverage to the value of human capital and the contribution of HR to the success of the business enterprise.

What should be the level of Human Capital ROI?

A natural and obvious question indeed. Like any other financial indicator, the level of HCROI should be a factor in your organization's business plan for the year. Once you know the current HCROI level you can plan to increase it by taking action to improve your organization's performance, just as sales would take actions to improve revenue, or operations would take actions to streamline and improve processes, thereby lowering operating costs and improving EBITDA.

Human Resources' plans for increased HCROI should support the business' financial goals. As an example, if you are measuring HCROI for several business units, a goal could be to move each business unit's HCROI to that of the highest performing business unit, over time.

Another question that may be asked by the CEO, board member, or investor is: what level of HCROI should we strive for? The answer to this question is the answer to the following question: what ROI, above the cost of capital (financial capital costs), does our company expect to generate on its investments? A CFO, CEO, or board member will readily know the answer to this question.

Measuring Productivity

Productivity measures the amount of revenue generated for each dollar invested in human capital, after adjusting for the costs of raw materials and financial capital costs. This formula is an adaptation of the traditional financial measure for productivity (Revenue ÷ Assets), and it normalizes all types of business models (those driven by products versus services) by controlling for raw material costs, which vary greatly by industry. It is necessary to normalize for raw material costs because material costs can distort the productivity value of human capital. By subtracting raw materials, you are able to capture how much value-added revenue people drive, as explained in the value-added section.

Applying these concepts, here is the formula to measure Human Capital Productivity:

$$\text{HC Productivity} = \frac{\text{Revenue} - \text{Raw Material Costs}}{\text{Human Capital Investment} + \text{Financial Capital Costs}}$$

What should be the level of Productivity?

As with HCROI, the level of productivity should be a factor in your organization's business plan for the year. And again, once you know your current productivity you can plan to increase it by taking human capital strategy actions to improve your organization's performance.

As with HCROI, the CEO, board member, or investor may ask: what level of productivity should we strive for? Again, a more useful question is: what level of productivity will produce the desired level of HCROI?

Liquidity or Profit Sensitivity

Profit Sensitivity is a liquidity metric that measures the ratio between profit-*driven* incentive compensation and a profit goal for the company. This formula is an adaptation of the financial metric, quick ratio, also known as the acid test, used to measure liquidity. The quick ratio is the most stringent method used by finance professionals to determine if liquidity levels are sufficient to protect an organization's cash position.

The Profit Sensitivity metric is a corollary of the acid test, but with a laser focus on the organization's compensation structure. The formula's premise is that incentive compensation is the most agile tool a business can use to protect its profitability. A high Profit Sensitivity value shows that incentive compensation can help maintain a stable earnings pattern, thereby protecting the value of the enterprise.

Applying these concepts, here is the formula to measure profit sensitivity or liquidity:

$$\text{Profit Sensitivity} = \frac{\text{Profit-}\textit{Driven}\text{ Incentive Compensation Plan}}{\text{EBITDA Plan}}$$

Budgeted or Plan profit-driven incentive compensation is the sum of those compensation elements in the annual financial plan, linked to the profitability of the company. This would include incentive pay, profit-sensitive employer matches on 401 (k) plans, and LTI awards based on company profitability. EBITDA Plan is the amount of EBITDA contemplated in the annual financial plan. These amounts would be set when the annual financial plan is finalized for the fiscal year. While it is common to adjust the financial plan during the fiscal year, we suggest that the Profit Sensitivity calculation be changed only on an annual basis. The point of this value is to establish the relationship and then assess its appropriateness.

This method of viewing incentive compensation is a novel approach. The typical relationship for incentive compensation among compensation practitioners is percentage of base compensation. An annual or long-term incentive plan sets "targets" that are a function of base compensation. Competitive practice greatly influences the level, scope, performance targets, and other features of incentive compensation programs.

As noted above, we suggest an additional relationship be considered, the relationship of incentive/variable compensation to profits. This relationship is introduced in a June 2005 *Harvard Business Review* article "The Surprising Economics of a "People Business" (Felix Barber and Rainer Strack of Boston Consulting Group). Barber and Strack observed that variable compensation can significantly reduce the volatility of earnings and thus make a company more attractive to investors by reducing their risk. Even small changes in the level and structure of compensation can have a major impact on the level of profits, especially in companies where human capital costs represent a large portion of total operating costs.

In *The Workforce Scorecard*, the authors (Mark Huselid, Brian Becker and Richard Beatty) list Five Key Principles for Developing Workforce Measures. Principle III is: *Think in Terms of Relationships Among Metrics Before You Think About the Levels of the Metrics.* In short, while the level of a measure is important, relationships give a context for understanding what the appropriate measurement target ought to be.

This concept is implicit in the design and expensing of a typical incentive compensation program. The proof? Watch what happens to incentive compensation accruals during the fiscal year as profitability emerges. If profits are tracking below plan, the incentive compensation pool accrual is reduced and vice versa.

This relationship also informs management precisely on the degree of profit protection, if business results don't unfold as planned. Moreover, by highlighting this relationship, one would fully expect that having a measure such as Profit Sensitivity will lead boards and management alike to ask some very basic questions about the scope and extent of incentive compensation beyond the traditional dimensions of relationship to base pay and competitive practice.

By measuring total incentive compensation in relation to the fiscal plan profit, and managing to a desired relationship, the volatility of earnings will be lower and risks will be reduced, thereby making the company more attractive to investors.

Productivity and HCROI Correlation

As shown in the chart below, there is a positive correlation between productivity and human capital ROI. Generally, the higher the level of productivity, the higher the level of ROI. Thus, if an organization wants to improve its return on human capital it needs to improve productivity. The results are for a financial services company comparing the HCROI and productivity of six homogeneous geographic regions across the United States. This example shows a wide variance in both HCROI and productivity.

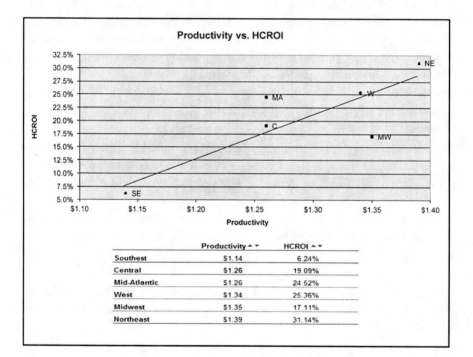

	Productivity ▲▼	HCROI ▲▼
Southeast	$1.14	6.24%
Central	$1.26	19.09%
Mid-Atlantic	$1.26	24.52%
West	$1.34	25.36%
Midwest	$1.35	17.11%
Northeast	$1.39	31.14%

The above methods to measure the ROI, productivity and liquidity (profit sensitivity) of the human capital investment will answer the challenge posed by the CEO. The results of these formulas will show the CEO and the board the value the investment in human capital is adding to the business enterprise. Moreover, these methods provide HR with hard numbers that can be produced regularly and rapidly, and make the so-called business case for the changes in human capital strategy to continuously improve business performance. The formulas have been developed in collaboration with and vetted by discriminating CFOs, private equity executives, and investment bankers, so they'll pass the CFO smell test. In short, the data and formulas meet the Seven Guiding Principles.

CHAPTER 3

A HUMAN CAPITAL STRATEGY MODEL

"What gets measured, gets done."

— Ram Charan

In Chapter Two, we examined a rationale for and explained a set of formulas for calculating the ROI, productivity and liquidity of the entire investment in human capital, defined as employee costs, costs in support of employees and costs in lieu of employees. To calculate the values, all of the data are sourced from the financial system; the most trusted and often audited company data.

Having "hard numbers" is good, but of little value for this purpose, unless one knows what to do with the numbers to improve business performance. The next three chapters of this book will focus on the process of converting the hard numbers into human capital strategy actions that will result in higher productivity, leading to higher human capital ROI and enhanced value of the business.

BUSINESS STRATEGY MODEL: HC-CENTRIC VS. STRUCTURE-CENTRIC

A human capital strategy is an integral element of a business strategy. Following is an illustration of a business strategy model, including its major components.

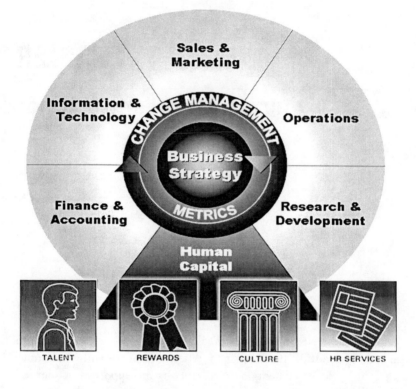

This illustration shows not only the major elements of a business strategy but also a set of metrics, which are needed, as stressed earlier, in all aspects of the business to measure performance. Business strategies, by their nature, are living environments. As such, they are in a state of constant change, thus the need for a vibrant and robust milieu for the effective management of steady changes. This also applies to human capital strategy.

In *Talent: Making People Your Competitive Advantage*, Ed Lawler notes that the business strategies of organizations are either structure-centric or HC-centric. Structure-centric companies can organize either as a *hierarchical bureaucracy* or as a *low-cost operator*. Over the years structure-centric organizations have been losing market share and are likely to continue to lose market share. Lawler argues it is reasonable to put aside the hierarchical bureaucracy approach as it simply is not an effective way to organize and manage most businesses. As we continue to move to a knowledge-based economy, the majority of employees require high levels of expertise to do their jobs, innovation will be critical to compete effectively, and meeting customers' demands will require employees in various parts of the organization to work together effectively and seamlessly. Quite simply, hierarchical management systems just don't work effectively in this environment.

A HC-centric organization, on the other hand, is one that aligns its features toward the creation of working relationships that attract talented individuals and enable them to work together in an effective manner. For companies that are competing on innovative products and services for which employee contact with customers is central, an HC-centric approach is essential to sustainable business success. Here are some of the features of an HC-centric organization:

- *Business strategy is determined by talent considerations, and it in turn drives human capital management practices.*

- *Every aspect of the organization is focused on talent and talent management.*

- *Performance management is one of the most important activities of the organization.*

- *The information system gives the same amount of attention and rigor to measures of talent costs, performance, and condition as it does to measures of equipment, materials, buildings, supplies, and financial assets.*

- *The HR department is the most important staff group.*

- *The corporate board has both the expertise and the information it needs to understand and advise on talent issues.*

- *Leadership is shared, and managers are highly skilled in talent management.*

Interestingly, Lawler argues that talent considerations drive business strategy, contrary to conventional wisdom that suggests that business strategy should drive talent considerations.

Lawler is not alone in this view. In Jim Collins' seminal book *Good to Great*, Collins and his research team concluded that for companies to achieve breakthrough results they first need to get the right people on the bus, the wrong people off the bus, and the right people in the right seats. Only then can they figure out where to drive the bus. This principle is referred to as **First Who... Then What.** Collins also asserts that the old adage "people are our most important asset" is wrong. People are not your most important asset. The *right* people are.

Yet another business strategist joins this chorus of people before business strategy. Jeffrey Pfeffer writes in *The Human Equation* that senior managers of the most successful companies worry more about their people and about learning, skill, and competence in their organizations than they do about having the right strategy. Pfeffer goes on to say that the real sources of competitive leverage are the culture and capabilities of an organization that are derived from how people are managed. To prove this point, Pfeffer demonstrates through numerous credible studies that revenue growth didn't drive shareholder value; nor was size an indicator of business success. Neither industry nor downsizing determined value. Pfeffer concludes that people are the consistent point of differentiation and the ultimate driver of enterprise value.

Robert Waterman of *In Search of Excellence* fame observed that "people are the strategy." The successful companies Waterman researched do look for sustainable competitive advantage, but they get it from the way they organize, not from a brilliant idea. Because they persist where others give up, they accomplish the most difficult part of strategy, implementation. Success comes from successfully implementing strategy, not just from having one. This implementation capability derives, in large measure, from the organization's people, how they are treated, their skills and competencies, and their efforts on behalf of the organization.

These distinguished authors offer compelling evidence that the people strategy of the business is not only a vital element of a business strategy, it should drive business strategy. As established above, people, how they are organized and work together ultimately determine the success of a business.

HUMAN CAPITAL STRATEGY ELEMENTS

A human capital strategy consists of four major elements: **Talent, Rewards, Culture, and HR Services.** I'll explain shortly why we have these four elements, but first some context.

When one asks: What does a human capital strategy consist of? A typical response is a litany of HR programs: performance management, leadership development, compensation, benefits, HRIS, and so on. Many who have written books in this area focus on the importance of various aspects of a human capital strategy to improve business performance, but none define what is included in a concise, comprehensive, and cohesive human capital strategy.

My firm, Vienna Human Capital Advisors, is an HR consultancy that provides strategic advice on all aspects of human capital strategy, linked to and aligned with the business strategy. We hire former chief human resource officers (CHROs) that are adept at configuring HR strategies to effectively meet the goals of the business. I mention this, not to plug my firm, but to provide a foundation for all that is included in a human capital strategy.

I need to point out one other piece of my background to explain the context of the four elements. In my days as a benefits consultant, my colleagues and I often encountered clients or prospects that wanted to hire a consultant to help them redesign a pension plan, or a 401(k) plan, or a health care program, or an executive benefit plan, or a whatever. Sometimes what they requested was precisely what they needed and we did our very best to meet their objectives for the program.

However, all too often, we were concerned that the solution the company had in mind would not solve the particular problem they described. For example, we were often given these reasons for the need to overhaul a particular program: high turnover, inability to attract talent, productivity problems of the workforce, low employee engagement scores. Frequently, upon deeper analysis, we would discover that the root causes of the problem were factors other than the adequacy of the benefit program. The causes included a tyrannical manager causing turnover and low engagement scores, lack of a comprehensive development program for up-and-coming talent, a compensation system that did not effectively reward outstanding achievement, or a cultural environment that fostered dynamic tension when collegial collaboration was needed. In these situations, the solution the client or prospect had in mind was only a small portion of the ultimate solution required.

I came to appreciate that most of the people issues hindering business success are multidimensional in nature and as such require a multifaceted response. Thus, one needed experience and expertise in multiple aspects of human capital strategy to accurately diagnose the nature of a people problem in order to effectively propose the right set of strategies to solve it.

As we were developing the Vienna HCA concept (strategic HR consultancy), we knew we needed to be able to answer the question: What is a human capital strategy? We also knew the answer was not a litany of programs and processes. The challenge was finding a way to categorize this litany of programs and processes in a concise, comprehensive, and cohesive manner. As we went through the process of compiling the material, we saw themes that led us to what we've come to describe as the four elements of a human capital strategy. Again, they are Talent, Rewards, Culture, and HR Services.

TALENT

In *The War for Talent*, authors Ed Michaels, Helen Handfield-Jones, and Beth Axelrod, define talent as the sum of a person's abilities–his or her intrinsic gifts, skills, knowledge, experience, intelligence, judgment, attitude, character, and drive. It also includes the ability to learn and grow.

Consistent with this definition, the Talent dimension of a human capital strategy defines the background, skills, and competencies of the people needed to achieve an organization's mission, vision, and goals. It also defines the types of programs necessary to meet the development needs of employees and prescribes performance standards that will guide employees in their day-to-day activities. Here is a list of the major items included in the Talent dimension:

- Organization design. This is the architecture of the organization. Who reports to whom? This is not the sole province of human resources, but HR should have a perspective on how best to organize the business to achieve its mission and goals.

- Strategic staffing plan. Some refer to this as workforce planning. Think of this as Jim Collins' 2nd principle: First Who...Then What (Right people on the bus, in the right seats). Strategic staffing is the systematic identification and analysis of what an organization is going to need in terms of size, type, and quality of workforce to achieve its objectives. It determines what mix of experience, knowledge, skills, and competencies are required and sequences steps to get the right number of people in the right place at the right time.

- Staffing. This is the process of finding and attracting the right talent for the organization consistent with the strategic staffing plan. This is the function within an organization responsible for recruitment, screening, and selection of employees.

- Diversity. Diversity is the collective mixture of differences and similarities of individuals and of the organization that encompasses values, beliefs, experiences, backgrounds, preferences, and behaviors.

- Leadership and professional development. This is the process of defining the development needs of the people in the organization, in order for them to perform at a high level. This takes multiple forms from individual coaching to broad-based didactic instruction for the group.

- Performance management. This is the process of managing or improving employee job performance through the use of performance assessment tools, coaching, and counseling as well as providing continuous feedback.

- Succession planning. This is the process of identifying long-range needs and cultivating a supply of internal talent to meet those future needs. It is used to anticipate the future needs of the organization and assist in finding, assessing, and developing the human capital necessary to the strategy of the organization.

The talent dimension of the human capital strategy is a rapidly evolving field due to the current extraordinarily dynamic business environment. This is driven by accelerated changes in business models (i.e., Blockbuster to Netflix or bookstores to Amazon), globalization, outsourcing, technology, challenging shareholder demands, and evolving workforce cultures and expectations dictated by a new generation of employees.

Peter Cappelli in *Talent on Demand* (2008) describes the end of an era that was driven by so-called academy companies with chess masters moving candidates around the equivalent of the chessboard of the organization chart. We are no longer, nor have we been, in *The Organization Man* period where the company decided which candidates were ready for which jobs to meet its longer-term talent needs. In today's world, employees more or less control their own career destiny. Commitment to a single organization for one's career is virtually unheard of. Companies' talent strategies need to be highly agile to respond to these dynamic market conditions. Thus, while all of the elements of a talent strategy are vital to a comprehensive talent strategy, the form they take will vary from company to company and even among divisions within the same company, in response to each division's unique business circumstances.

REWARDS

The Rewards dimension of the human capital strategy defines how employees and staff will be compensated for their efforts and contributions toward achieving the organization's mission, vision and goals. This includes both pay and benefits. Here is a list of the major items included in the Rewards dimension:

- Base compensation – An amount or a rate of compensation for a specified position of employment or activity excluding any other payments or allowances.

- Sales compensation – A compensation system designed for individuals employed in managerial sales or sales representative positions. Individuals are paid on a commission or percentage-of-sale basis, in correlation with the achievement of specified sales goals. Sales compensation may be paid in addition to or in lieu of Base compensation.

- Annual incentive compensation – Variable pay that recognizes team and individual performance typically paid in a lump sum in the form of cash or a combination of cash and stock. The annual incentive plan is usually the most variable of the compensation elements, with the cost of the plan in a particular year flexing up and down with the aggregate achievement of incentive goals by participants.

- Long-term incentive compensation – These programs are typically stock-based and reflect the entire organization's success over a multiple-year period.

- Employee benefits – These programs include such items as health insurance, life insurance, disability income insurance, a pension and/or a 401(k) type of program, and time off with pay (holidays and vacation). The designs of these programs are typically influenced by competitive practice and they are heavily regulated at both the federal and state level, and in limited cases at the municipal level.

- Perquisites – Executive perquisites represent another component of the total compensation package. Perquisites are generally cash, property or services that an organization provides to executives in addition to salary. The more common executive perquisites include a company car or car allowance, club membership dues, financial counseling, physical exams, and home computers.

All of the Reward elements need to be consistent with and advance the business strategy, plus they need to consistent with each other and the values of the business.

CULTURE

Culture is the composite of individual employee behaviors and how people work together as teams. Marvin Bower, for years managing director of McKinsey & Company and author of *The Will to Manage*, offered this informal definition of business culture—"the way we do things around here." Culture ties people together and gives meaning and purpose to their day-to-day lives, or not.

The culture of a business reflects the underlying values, beliefs, and principles that serve as the foundation for an organization's management system, along with the set of management practices and behaviors that both exemplify and reinforce those basic principles.

Values are the bedrock of any corporate culture. As the essence of a company's philosophy for achieving success, values provide a sense of common direction for all employees and guidelines for their day-to-day behavior.

A values statement is an expression of a company's core beliefs. Companies write the statement to identify and connect with the employees, customers, and suppliers. Additionally, the declaration allows for the company's staff to be aware of the priorities and goals of the company. For example, a company might list one of its guiding principles as "Customer service is priority one."

Organizations gain great strength from shared values—with emphasis on the "shared." If employees know what their company stands for, if they know what standards they are to uphold, then they are much more likely to make decisions that will support those standards. They are also more likely to feel as if they are an important part of the organization. They are motivated because life in the company has meaning for them. Because organizational values can powerfully influence what people actually do, values ought to be a matter of great concern to managers and leaders. In fact, shaping and enhancing values can become the most important job a manager or leader can do.

How do shared values affect organizational performance? In broad terms, they act as an informal control system that tells people what is expected of them.

HR is the keeper of the values flame for the organization. HR typically leads employee survey projects that in part measure the extent to which employees live the values the organization espouses. HR also plays a major role in communicating the organization values.

Throughout my consulting career I would hear that the need for a change in benefit strategy was being driven by a cultural inconsistency. In fact, culture was a major factor for the adoption of flexible compensation programs and 401(k) plans. As companies became less paternalistic, they wanted to give employees greater control over how they received their compensation, and flex programs and 401(k) plans did exactly that.

The organization's values and culture also extend to and influence greatly all aspects of the Talent strategy. The design of the organization structure (hierarchical vs. lattice), the nature and type of people to recruit, how employees are developed, managed, and selected for leadership positions all need to sync with the values and culture of the organization.

I'll conclude this section on values with a story that vividly illustrates the linkage of culture and human capital strategy. I once worked with a firm that publishes a prominent monthly magazine distributed worldwide. The organization had recently hired a new CEO to reverse the financial fortunes of the struggling publication. My company, Foster Higgins, was retained to help the CEO restructure the employee benefit program.

In the project kickoff meeting, the CEO waxed eloquently about the need to change the culture of the organization if there was any hope to reverse business fortunes. Up to that point, the culture had been very paternalistic; in fact, employees were given off every Friday during the month of May to enjoy the blossoms of spring. The CEO wanted to transition from a culture of paternalism to one of accountability. The three most dramatic changes in the employee benefit program included:

1. Discontinuing the Fridays-in-May holidays

2. Elimination of a defined benefit pension plan, paid for entirely by the company and replaced with a 401(k) requiring employee contributions to receive an employer contribution that also included a supplemental profit sharing contribution, if defined financial goals were achieved.

3. Requiring employees to make contributions for health insurance coverage for them and their families, previously paid entirely by the company.

There were numerous other changes in the benefits area as well as in the compensation program. On the surface, these changes demanded more of the employees, yet they made them feel more in control of their own success and that of the company. By the way, the changes enacted by this company worked. The publication today is financially vibrant.

HR SERVICES

The HR Services dimension of the human capital strategy defines what the Human Resources Department should be doing to assist the organization in achieving its mission, vision, and goals. As a department that serves the needs of employees and management, it must be structured and staffed in a manner that will allow it to meet its customers' needs quickly, efficiently, and satisfactorily.

The HR function also needs to play a leading role in driving the organization's entire human capital strategy. Unfortunately, this is all too often a missed opportunity for HR. Recently, Vienna was retained by the CEO of a large multisite healthcare system in New England to help the system develop a new, comprehensive, human capital strategy, aligned with a new strategy for its business. The CEO sought Vienna's help because the incumbent CHRO wasn't up to the task. While highly regarded as a capable employee champion and labor relations expert, he lacked the strategic partner competency.

The major items in the HR services strategy include:

- The staffing function, responsible for finding and recruiting the talent needed to achieve the business strategy
- The development function, responsible for workforce planning, training and development of employees, performance management, and succession planning
- The compensation function, responsible for the base salary configuration, annual incentives, and the long-term incentive program
- The employee benefits function, responsible for the design, funding, and administration of the employee benefits program

- The employee relations function, responsible for assessing, designing, developing, and implementing programs and policies to enhance employee morale and well-being
- The HRIS function, responsible for the data and information operations of the human resources department

In each of these respective functions, HR needs to maintain a set of metrics that measure the performance (quality, timeliness, and cost) of the function. We will discuss these metrics in Chapter Four.

In summary, people *are* the business, and the single most vital ingredient in defining a business strategy. For this reason, a comprehensive and cohesive human capital strategy is critical to the success of the enterprise. For the human capital strategy to achieve its potential, all of the elements of the strategy must be properly synchronized and supported throughout the organization. When this harmony is achieved, an organization is well positioned to achieve its goals.

CHAPTER 4

TRANSLATING NUMBERS INTO STRATEGY

"The hallmark of any highly effective organization is making good decisions and making them better, faster and more consistently than their competitors."

— Paul Rogers and Marcia Blenko,
Bain & Company

This chapter provides a comprehensive, cohesive process to translate the human capital ROI and productivity results into specific changes in human capital strategy that will lead to improving both human capital financial results and overall business results.

But before we get into the process, a slight diversion. Recently, there was a LinkedIn discussion in the Business Analytic Group entitled: "What's the elevator sales pitch for analytics?" Here is a sampling of some of the responses:

- Business analytics is the process that transforms raw data into actionable strategic knowledge to guide decisions aiming to increase market share, revenue, and profit.

- It is an analytic process that transforms raw data into actionable insights, the true transformation from "So what?" to "Now what?"

- (It goes) from data to decision making.

- Analytics is about seizing opportunities for competitive advantage by leveraging insight hidden in data. If the CEO and board are interested in generating revenue, mitigating risk and reducing cost in their organization, then investing in analytics will position them competitively and help them seize opportunities with greater precision.

- Fact-based decision making gives you a competitive edge. Better data > better analysis > better decisions > increased ROI.

At Vienna HCA we define human capital analytics as the process of measuring and analyzing the investment in human capital (people). Measuring identifies how well the investment in human capital is performing. The analysis scrutinizes the results and identifies the changes necessary in human capital strategy that will continuously improve the return on the human capital investment, thereby enhancing the economic value of the business enterprise.

In sum, the analytic process is about making business decisions with a higher level of precision that lead to better business results.

Now, onto the process of translating human capital ROI and productivity results into strategic actions. In short, the process can be broken down in this way:

1. Dissect and analyze the human capital ROI and productivity formula elements to understand the factors driving results.

2. Analyze HR metrics that will help identify the factors driving the ROI and productivity results.

3. Probe, in collaboration with business managers, the factors driving financial results, and identify the human capital strategy changes necessary to continuously improve productivity, human capital ROI, and overall business performance.

4. Write the story that explains why the results are the way they are, and describes the changes necessary to improve the results, and the resources required (people, time, and money) to fully develop and implement the solutions.

5. Get CEO's and business leaders' approvals to execute necessary changes.

ANALYZING HUMAN CAPITAL ROI AND PRODUCTIVITY RESULTS

The first step in understanding the human capital ROI and productivity results is to break them down into the formula's component parts. For human capital ROI the components are EBITDA, financial capital costs, and human capital costs/investments. The component parts for productivity are revenue, raw material costs, human capital, and financial capital costs.

All of these numbers need to be compared to the budget/business plan and tracked over sequential time periods. In addition, human capital costs, financial capital costs, EBITDA, and raw material costs, if any, need to be compared to revenue to determine positive and negative trends. This exercise will isolate the financial factors driving the results.

A case study will illustrate the effectiveness of this approach. A client in the construction industry had a significant drop-off of human capital ROI and productivity, despite rapidly growing revenue. Here is a table showing the results of the analysis.

Time Period/Results	Year 1	Year 2	Change ($&%)
Human Capital ROI	15.6%	1.9%	(88%)
Productivity	$1.41	$1.34	(5%)
Revenue	$188.7 million	$235.9 million	$47.2 million 25%
Raw Material (Dollars and % of Revenue)	$64.2 million 34%	$90.5 million 38.4%	$26.3 million 41%
Human Capital Costs (Dollars and % of Revenue)	$77.8 million 41.2%	$96.3 million 40.9%	$18.5 million 23.8%
Financial Capital Costs (Dollars and % of Revenue)	$10.4 million 5.5%	$12.6 million 5.3%	$2.2 million 21.2%
EBITDA (Dollars and % of Revenue)	$22.5 million 11.9%	$14.4 million 6.9%	($8.1 million) (36%)

As the data in this example shows, revenue, human capital costs and financial capital costs increased in the low to mid 20% in year two, whereas raw material costs increased 41%, and EBITDA declined by $8.1 million or 36%. It turned out that the cost of raw material was increasing at a rapid, disproportionate rate due to the price of oil, yet the company did not reflect the increased raw material costs in their pricing of projects. Thus, EBITDA declined, driving down human capital ROI, and raw material costs increased, driving down productivity. While this is a dramatic example, it vividly illustrates the value of dissecting the results to understand what factor or factors are driving them. Because the company was able to isolate the factors driving the reduction in human capital ROI and productivity they implemented both human capital and business process changes to effectively address these results.

On the next two pages are two dashboards that illustrate the human capital ROI and productivity results over time, and against financial plan in a concise and coherent manner that can be used in the C-suite.

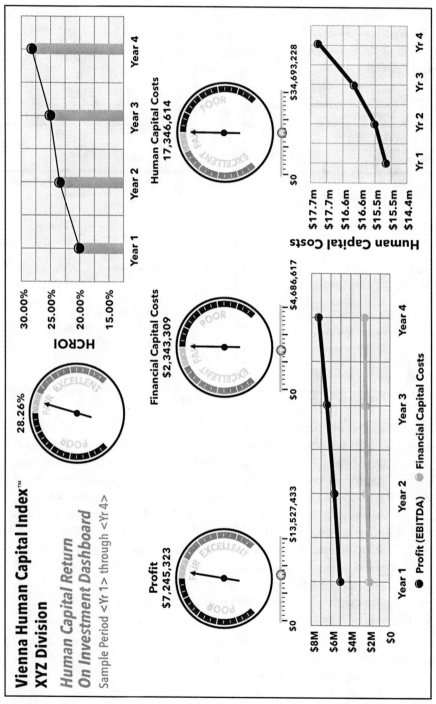

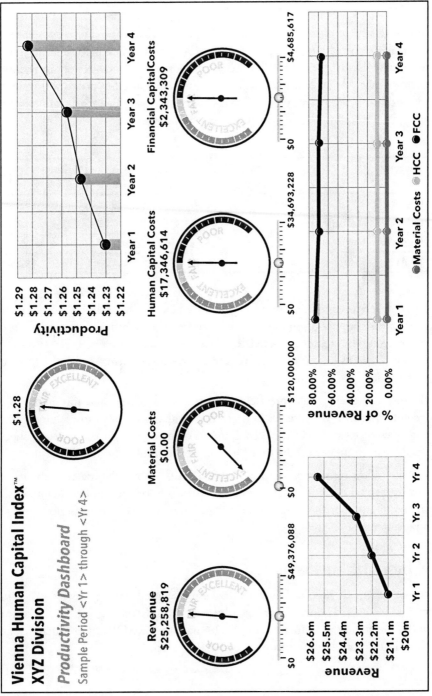

The next step in dissecting the human capital ROI and productivity results is to break down the human capital costs by category and line item to understand what specific categories and line items are positively or negatively impacting performance. As an example, the table below, from another client, illustrates a significant increase in human capital costs driven largely by increases in costs in support of employees and costs in lieu of employees.

Category	Year 1 (% of Revenue)	Year 2 (% of Revenue)	% change
Employee Costs	38.8%	39.1%	1.0%
Costs in Support of Employees	5.1%	7.1%	39.2%
Costs in Lieu of Employees	16.5%	22.3%	35.2%
Total Costs	**60.4%**	**68.5%**	**13.4%**

Upon deeper investigation into the general ledger line items driving the increase in costs in support of employees, we discovered a significant increase in real estate costs, due to renegotiated lease rates for housing employees. The large increase in costs in lieu of employees was driven by contingent labor provided by a vendor.

Because the client could precisely identify the categories and line items that were driving relative increases in costs, the company was able to design specific strategies that would get these costs under control. The implemented changes would lead to higher productivity and improved human capital ROI.

On the following page is another dashboard that shows the major elements of human capital costs (employee costs, costs in support of employees, and costs in lieu of employees) compared to budget, over successive time periods and as a percentage of revenue.

ANALYZING HR METRICS

As we explained in Chapter Three, a human capital strategy consists of four major elements: Talent, Rewards, Culture, and HR Services. To help determine and understand the factors driving the human capital ROI and productivity, an organization can look to its own set of HR metrics.

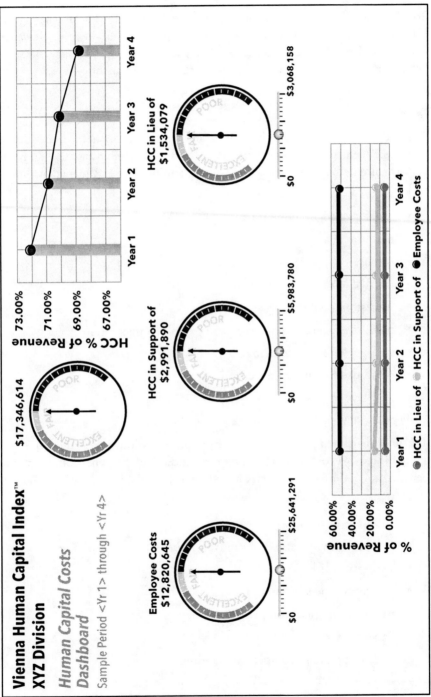

Vienna Human Capital Index™
XYZ Division

Human Capital Costs
Dashboard
Sample Period <Yr 1> through <Yr 4>

HCC % of Revenue

73.00%
71.00%
69.00%
67.00%

Year 1   Year 2   Year 3   Year 4

$17,346,614

POOR
EXCELLENT FAIR

HCC in Lieu of
$1,534,079

POOR
EXCELLENT FAIR

$0 $3,068,158

HCC in Support of
$2,991,890

POOR
EXCELLENT FAIR

$0 $5,983,780

Employee Costs
$12,820,645

POOR
EXCELLENT FAIR

$0 $25,641,291

% of Revenue

60.00%
40.00%
20.00%
0.00%

Year 1   Year 2   Year 3   Year 4

● HCC in Lieu of   ● HCC in Support of   ● Employee Costs

To add some coherency to the process, there is logical merit to organizing the HR metrics along the lines of the human capital strategy–Talent, Rewards, Culture, and HR Services. To that end, here are some of the HR measures we believe offer the greatest potential value in each of the four categories.

Talent

The talent dimension of the human capital strategy consists of: organization design, strategic staffing, staffing function, diversity, leadership and development, performance management, and succession planning. The HR metrics include:

- vacancy rates
- staffing configuration ratios
- new hire quality
- turnover,
- internal job fills
- succession pool coverage
- training expense as a percentage of payroll/compensation
- average performance rating
- distribution of performance ratings

Rewards

The rewards dimension consists of base compensation, sales compensation, annual incentive compensation, long-term incentive compensation, employee benefits, and perquisites. The HR metrics in this category include:

- Base pay, % of revenue
- 1099s, % of revenue
- Profit sensitivity, ratio of incentive compensation to EBITDA
- % of pay at risk,
- Market compensation ratio
- Benefit costs, % of compensation
- Benefit costs, % of revenue
- Benefits program, competitive standing

Culture

The culture dimension consists of the values and desired behaviors of the organization. The HR metrics in this category include:

- Employee engagement scores
- Employee exit survey results
- Client satisfaction ratings

HR Services

The HR Services dimension of the human capital strategy evaluates the services provided by the HR function for its constituents. In short, it answers the question: Is HR delivering quality services in a timely manner at a reasonable cost? The scope of the services includes staffing, organization development, compensation and benefits, employee relations, and HR technology. The HR metrics in this category include:

- HR department customer satisfaction,
- HR staffing ratio
- HR budget, as a % of revenue
- Time to fill
- Recruiting efficiency
- Quality of hire
- Training effectiveness index
- HR operations cycle times
- HR operations error rates

A Case Example

Analyzing these and other HR metrics will help the organization gain an understanding of the people factors driving the results. In addition, when used in collaboration with the financial analysis described above, a compelling, credible picture begins to form explaining why the HCROI and productivity results are what they are.

To illustrate this point, Chapter Two included a regression chart showing the distribution of productivity and HCROI among six homogeneous business units in a particular company. The ROI ranged from a low of 6.24% to a high of 31.14%, while productivity ranged from a low of $1.14 to a high of $1.39. Following the method described in this chapter, we discovered that human capital costs were driving the poor performance in the lowest performing business unit. Human capital costs were 76.1% of revenue versus 60.9% for the best performing unit. Moreover, all three elements of human capital costs (employee costs, costs in support of employees, and costs in lieu of employees) were high. Digging further, we discovered that base salaries as a percentage of revenue, incentive compensation, real estate costs, and contingent labor costs were the culprits driving the high costs. We further discovered, through a review of a limited HR metrics data set, that there was a significant staffing configuration issue, turnover was too low, and several vacancies existed in key positions. With this information, we were prepared to undertake the next step in the process to develop the necessary changes in human capital strategy to improve overall business performance.

INTERVIEWING BUSINESS MANAGERS

While everything done up to this point is necessary in order to understand, from HR's perspective, the factors driving results; the crucial next step in the process is interviewing business managers to get their perspectives on the root causes driving performance and what can be done from a human capital strategy perspective to improve productivity and thus human capital ROI. To get the buy-in necessary for the changes needed to improve performance, business manager perspectives are vital!

High-quality interactions between people with complementary knowledge are an integral part of the human capital strategy process. Dean Spitzer, PhD writes in his book *Transforming Performance Measurement* "the data-to-knowledge-to-wisdom conversion process reflects one of the great positives of transformational measurement. Although it is possible for individuals to do this alone, the most effective way to create knowledge and wisdom from measurement is through frequent and high-quality interactions between people with complementary knowledge. Ask anybody (including yourself): 'Do you learn more from data or from interacting with other people who have a like-minded mission.' It is ultimately the *social things* that will help convert measurement from information into knowledge and wisdom and, in the process, positively transform the context of measurement."

The first step in the process of interviewing business managers is to create an interview guide which would begin with a review of the HCROI and productivity results, analysis of the HCROI and productivity results, and analysis of the HR metrics results to partially explain, through the numbers, what is driving the results. These findings should be outlined for the company as a whole and the business unit individually. Depending on the culture of the company, it may also make sense to compare the results of the business unit to its peers.

To be consistent with the process for organizing the HR metrics, the interview guide should be structured along the four dimensions of the human capital strategy: Talent, Rewards, Culture, and HR Services. Here are some of the possible topics that can be probed with the business managers. Some or all of these questions would be supplemented with references to the HCROI, productivity, and HR data to give hard context for the issues being probed.

Talent

- Organization design: Does the current organization structure support your business needs?
- Strategic staffing: Do you have the right people in the right jobs?
- Organization development: Do your people have the right skills and competencies needed to perform at a high level? If not, what types of development programs are needed?
- Succession planning: The proverbial hit by the bus scenario, who would step into your shoes? What about your direct reports? Are they ready? If not, what do we need to do to get them ready?
- Performance assessment: Is the existing performance management program driving the behaviors necessary to continuously improve business performance?

Rewards

- Compensation: Does the compensation program (base pay, annual and long-term incentives) help you recruit and retain the people you need to meet or exceed your business goals? If not, in what ways does it need to change?
- Benefits program: Does the benefit program help you recruit and retain the people you need to meet or exceed your business goals? If not, in what ways does it need to change?

Culture

- Values: Are the company values integrated adequately in your business unit? If not, what needs to be done? Do any of the values need to change?

- Behaviors: Are employee behaviors with each other consistent with the company values? Are employee behaviors with customers and supplier/vendors consistent with the company values?

HR Services

Are there things HR could be doing differently to better meet your needs? For instance, are there changes that HR can make that would improve the quality of HR service or cycle times?

The method of conducting the interviews would follow the SPDR method as described in the side bar.

TELLING THE STORY AND GETTING CEO APPROVAL

Over my consulting career I've encountered numerous situations where clients simply couldn't get their CEO buy-in to implement a program or an initiative that HR was convinced was necessary to improve business performance. How unfortunate, because most of the initiatives or programs had merit. I'm a victim of CEO rejection, as well; so, I know the feeling. No one wants to experience CEO or board rejection, at the very least it's emotionally deflating and at worst career ending.

As I reflected on my own experience and the client experiences I witnessed, I discovered the reason for the rejections was that the stories behind the recommended investments weren't compelling. In my case, I hadn't done my homework properly.

So what can be done to minimize the likelihood of CEO or board rejection in the context of human-capital-strategy-change recommendations? Tell a compelling story. No kidding! The question then is: What must a story include to make it compelling?

While every CEO is unique and every organization's culture distinct, the storyline that has a good chance of capturing the attention and support of the CEO and board is…increasing enterprise value. In the next chapter we will describe methods on how to calculate the impact on shareholder value of the changes in human capital strategy. For now, know that measuring the impact on shareholder value is vital to making a compelling business case.

To get there, the story needs to include:

- The HCROI and productivity results. Are the results on budget? Are they improving over time? Are there variances among divisions? What's driving the results? This is where the analysis described in the above sections is explained, including the input from the business leaders on the factors driving the results.

- The action plan. What are we going to do about it? What changes need to be made in human capital strategy that will improve the results? Here, the recommendations need to be so specific that even a CEO can comprehend the changes. In oh so many situations, I've had CEOs ask for practical examples of the implications of the recommended changes.

- Resource commitments. Describe how the changes are going to be implemented. Who's going to do the work? How long is it going to take? What is the budget and over what time period? Are the business managers committed to supporting the changes?

- Impact on shareholder value. If a CEO will agree to invest in the changes necessary to improve business performance, he/she will want to know the impact on shareholder value and how long it will take to achieve the results. Because the CEO's and other executives long-term incentive compensation (options, phantom, or restricted stock) is likely linked to share price, the CEO will be keenly interested in the magnitude of the impact and timing of the results.

While there are numerous techniques to presenting the story, the "tell them what you're going to tell them, tell them, tell them what you told them" method is quite effective in these types of presentations. For example, one time, when we started a presentation to the CFO (he was screening the pitch before it got to the CEO) by stating that we had a set of human capital strategy recommendations that would lead to an increase in shareholder value of $75 million, we captured his attention. We went on to tell him the HCROI and productivity results, explain the human capital strategy changes necessary to improve performance and the $2 million investment required over a three-year period. The end result, again, would be an increase in shareholder value of $75 million.

A RECURRING PROCESS

The entire approach described above should be a recurring activity to achieve the greatest ongoing effect. In summary, the recurring process consists of four major steps:

1. Measure. Calculate HCROI and productivity values, and collect the various HR metrics.

2. Analysis. Monitor trends and performance against the business plan or company standard, and among units. Discern the drivers of results.

3. Strategy Development. Recommend changes in human capital strategy to continuously improve results, specify the implementation plan (time and resources), and project the impact on shareholder value.

4. Strategy Execution. Implement the strategy changes according to plan.

TRUNCATING THE PROCESS

While the extensive process described here is intended to help companies identify the most appropriate changes in human capital strategy, it can and should be truncated based on each company's circumstances. For instance, we can all cite examples of company executives (HR, Operations, Finance, Marketing and Sales, and CEOs) who have keen and accurate insights on the precise factors driving performance and the most appropriate solutions. In such cases, it may not be necessary to follow the entire comprehensive and elaborate process as described in this model. Some steps may be eliminated or modified according to the particular circumstances and stage of development of your organization.

INTERNAL COMPARISONS

Internal comparisons of homogeneous business units typically are often the best tool for comparison to assess performance levels. While it is appropriate to measure the overall results for the business enterprise, internal comparisons among homogeneous units is a reasonable next step. CEOs and boards will find internal comparisons helpful as they will readily identify the business units in greatest need of deeper analysis and corrective actions. Also, deep knowledge of the factors that drive performance of homogeneous units may suggest which human capital strategies might be appropriate given good and bad performance among units.

GROWTH VS. ROI

An issue every company faces is where and how to invest. This is true with HR as well, as HR often makes investment recommendations. These recommendations typically relate to improving productivity of the HR staff and the overall work force.

It is also true that HR can and should make recommendations that directly drive business performance. In this regard, the primary question is, do we recommend investments in growth or ROI, or both simultaneously; and if so, how?

McKinsey and Co. has developed a margin/growth model that helps companies make informed business decisions about investing in growth (revenue) and managing margin (defined as return on invested capital [ROIC]), both vital to improving enterprise value. McKinsey's advice: Companies that already have high ROIC, should focus on raising revenues faster than the market. Conversely, if ROIC is below target: take actions to improve ROIC.

A corollary to the McKinsey model can be used for the human capital investment. Such corollary can be defined, as follows:

1. If human capital ROI (margin after financial capital costs) is above a target rate, and revenue growth below the growth target, invest in growth.

2. If human capital ROI is below a target rate, and revenue growth is above the growth target, manage human capital ROI improvement.

3. If human capital ROI and revenue growth are above their targets, invest in growth.

4. If human capital ROI and revenue growth are both below their respective targets, manage human capital ROI improvement.

As in the McKinsey model, the first priority is to manage the human capital investment so as to achieve an acceptable level of human capital ROI, then invest in growth.

The following graph illustrates how the McKinsey model was applied for a company whose human capital ROI was below target. Over a four year period the company lowered its overall human capital investment as a percentage of revenue to achieve an acceptable level of human capital ROI of 20%.

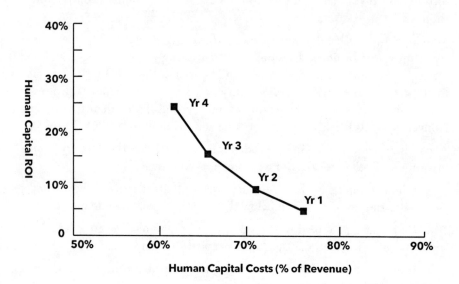

HUMAN CAPITAL STRATEGY MAP DIAGRAM

Appendix B provides a diagram that succinctly represents the human capital strategy development process.

HUMAN CAPITAL STRATEGY MAP WORKSHEET

Appendix C provides a worksheet that lays out an easy to follow process to record and analyze the human capital ROI, productivity, and HR metric results, the factors driving the results, and the human capital strategy actions necessary to improve results. Included in each section are areas to dissect the results and record observations.

In conclusion, knowing how well a company's investment in human capital is performing, while vital, is inadequate in and of itself. The real value that HR can bring to the CEO and board is its knowledge of what levers to push to continuously improve business performance. The methods described in this chapter, properly employed, will help HR identify the root causes of business performance issues, from a human capital perspective, and identify the right solutions to drive future performance. This process will not only help companies make better decisions, but they will do so faster and more consistently, as suggested by Rogers and Blenko of Bain & Company in the quote at the beginning of this chapter.

INTERVIEWING BUSINESS COLLEAGUES: THE SPDR METHOD

Having interviewed hundreds of executives over my consulting career and wanting some sense of order and effective discernment in the interview process, my colleagues and I developed an interview approach that fits nicely in the process of translating human capital financial results into human capital strategy actions. The approach is called SPDR; no, not the exchange traded funds (ETFs) products offered by State Street. This interviewing approach is short for:

- Spectrum of opportunity
- Practical implications
- Devil's advocacy
- Reconciliation

Spectrum of Opportunity

The interview method works as follows. Develop an interview guide, as described in this chapter, which asks a series of questions related to the potential issues causing poor human capital investment performance. The questions try to get at what human capital factors are driving the performance and the interviewer provides a spectrum of opportunity on potential solutions. For example, assume that the human capital ROI and productivity are below plan and trending in the wrong direction. Assume also that the HR metrics indicate there are low employee engagement scores and relatively high turnover in a particular division. The spectrum of opportunity interview question for the business leader could be posed as follows: "The productivity and human capital ROI in your division are below business plan and trending negatively. We also observed that the employee engagement scores are relatively low and turnover is relatively high. We're interested in your observations on what might be causing this level of performance and what actions we might take to improve the results. The spectrum of opportunity ranges from taking no actions to making far reaching, dramatic changes in the human capital strategy. What do you think should be done?" Presenting the data and strategic options in this manner will cause the business leader to offer their opinions on what, if any, actions are necessary to improve performance. Moreover, this method avoids any interviewer biases.

Practical Implications

Following this same example, after the business leader expresses their views on what actions to take, the interviewer describes the practical implications on the human capital strategy for that division so the business leader can see the practical consequences of the strategy changes. To illustrate, assume the business leader observes that the low engagement scores and high turnover are compensation-driven and base pay levels need to be increased. The interviewer would follow with a statement along the lines of…"Ok, we need to increase base salary levels X% which will improve future engagement scores and lower turnover, correct?" This process would be followed for all of the issues being explored.

Devil's Advocacy

Now the devil's advocacy…the interviewer challenges a potential negative outcome of the recommended changes to test the wisdom and validity of the solution. For example, in our hypothetical situation, the interviewer might say…"If we increase base salaries by X%, will that negatively impact your operating margin, and if so, is that an acceptable outcome?" In my experience, a business leader, when challenged in this fashion, will occasionally have second thoughts about the solution initially proposed. Even if their solution to the problem doesn't change, they'll be grateful a constructive, insightful challenge was offered.

Reconciliation

The final issue is reconciliation. This is where an insightful HR executive provides their greatest value to the process. During the course of the interview there will be many solutions discussed to respond to the many issues driving human capital investment performance. On occasion, not all of the solutions will fit together; and in fact, some of the solutions will work at cross purposes. It is the duty of the interviewer then to point out the discrepancies and ask the business leader to help resolve the inconsistency.

Here is an example of a situation with a company that was in need of human capital strategy reconciliation. The business leader of an underperforming division concluded the staffing configuration needed to be modified to drive growth. They needed to hire more sales staff. Also, to address a relatively high turnover issue, the business leader observed that it was necessary to raise base salaries. Both actions were certainly doable in and of themselves without an unacceptable impact on productivity or HCROI. However, the consequence of doing both simultaneously would result in a near-term, unacceptable reduction in productivity and human capital ROI. Acknowledging the need to reconcile this conflict, the business leader decided to hire more sales staff, because the need for revenue growth was a compelling imperative to the business. To address the turnover issue, the business leader increased incentive compensation for high performers and aggressively "transitioned" marginal performers, thereby generating the financial capital needed to fund higher base salaries and new hires while protecting the level of human capital ROI.

At the end of this process both the business leader and HR interviewer will have a common understanding, and hopefully agreement, on the changes in human capital strategy that will lead to improved financial performance of the business. Also, HR will have established a constructive method to engage business leaders in a dialogue on what needs to be done to improve financial results. Just as important to the process, HR and the business leaders agreeing on what shouldn't be done to improve performance.

The other benefit of this process is its recurring nature. As time and circumstances will prove, not all of the changes made in the human capital strategy will have the intended outcomes. In those situations the dialogue between the business leader and HR interviewer would go along the lines of…"Well, the level of productivity and human capital ROI still hasn't improved to an acceptable level as we expected, and the factors driving performance haven't materially changed. What other solutions might we consider to solve this problem? For instance, how about we try X, Y, or Z?"

CHAPTER 5

MEASURING THE IMPACT
OF HUMAN CAPITAL STRATEGY CHANGES
ON SHAREHOLDER VALUE

"What gets measured, gets managed."

– Peter Drucker

Though brief, this chapter is perhaps the most significant in the book, because we show how to credibly measure the impact of recommended changes in human capital strategy on shareholder value. Many like to claim that changes in human capital strategy will lead to improved profitability, but fail to show a credible path there, through the numbers. This chapter will provide that path in a clear and concise manner.

Quite simply, HR maximizes its influence in the C-suite and boardroom if it can credibly show how shareholder value will be affected by the changes in human capital strategy it recommends. This chapter will show how to calculate shareholder value impact for both publicly-traded and privately-held companies. This process has been vetted by very discriminating CFOs, investment bankers, and private equity executives and has passed their intense scrutiny.

MAKING THE BUSINESS CASE

Making the so-called business case–improved profits, thus justifying the resources commitment (money, people, and time)–is a necessary task in navigating the C-suite. Rarely does a CEO agree to invest in a significant change in human capital strategy if a solid business case hasn't been offered by the sponsor of the change. This is true in all aspects of a business, as it should be, not just HR. The more compelling the business case, the more likely the CEO will approve the necessary investment.

While improved profits are the goal for virtually any investment, the ultimate impact on shareholder value is of even greater consequence. Here's why. CEOs are judged by boards and shareholders on their influence on shareholder value, and their compensation is driven in large part by the extent to which they improve the value of the business. Look at the Compensation Discussion and Analysis (CD and A) section of any 10-K and you'll see that the CEO's total compensation is heavily weighted toward long-term incentives (LTI). LTI typically consists of some form of stock options or stock grants and their economic value is often several multiples of base pay and annual incentives. Now, put yourself in the CEO's shoes; what number is of greatest interest to you? Yes, it's stock price. Thus, by making a business case in the form of the impact on shareholder value you will readily have the attention of senior executives, boards, and shareholders.

There's another benefit to HR of presenting a business case in terms of shareholder value or stock price-credibility as a business partner. A widely held criticism of HR is that it lacks business acumen. The subtitle to Ram Charan's best-selling book *What the CEO Wants You To Know* is "Using Business Acumen to Understand How Your Company Really Works." HR is encouraged to think and act the same as the business people. Thinking in terms of shareholder value and what drives it from a human capital strategy perspective demonstrates business acumen.

Perhaps the most vivid illustration of the significance of stock price is what happened at a Dell Computers stockholders meeting several years ago. It may have been the shortest–and most effective–shareholder meeting ever. When founder and chairman Michael Dell took the stage, a slide comparing the performance of Dell's stock to companies such as Coca-Cola, Intel, and Microsoft appeared behind him. It took less than five seconds for the audience to realize that the upward slope labeled "Dell" was at least twice as steep as the ones for the other companies. Dell had outperformed these better-known companies by a wide margin. Just as the "oohs" and "aahs" from the appreciative shareholders reached their peak, Dell looked out at the audience and said, "And that concludes our presentation." The applause was deafening.

Here is a story that demonstrates the power of showing the impact on shareholder value of recommended changes in human capital strategy. A company in the financial services industry was growing very rapidly through acquisitions; however, organic growth was anemic. The head of one of the major business units was alarmed by this; he wanted to diagnose the root causes of the problem and develop a set of solutions that would drive substantial organic growth and improve the business operating margins. The business unit operated out of six homogeneous geographic regions, so there was, as Laurie Bassi of McBassi & Company defines it, an opportunity for a "naturally-occurring experiment" or credible internal comparisons.

A couple of the units were performing well financially while most were not. After extensive analysis, employing the methods described in Chapters Two, Three, and Four, the CHRO and business unit leader concluded that all aspects of human capital strategy (Talent, Rewards, Culture, and HR Services) needed to be modified in varying degrees, across the six geographic regions. The CHRO and the business unit leader determined they needed a budget commitment of about $2 million and two to three years time to effectively implement all the changes necessary to drive organic growth and significantly improve the overall financial results of the business unit.

The CHRO and the business leader made the business case by showing what the impact would be on shareholder value if all six units performed at the same level of margin (human capital ROI) as the best performing unit. Before the CHRO and business leader could present the business case to the CEO, they had to "run it by the CFO" to get the CFO's blessing on the numbers. As we all know, this is not unusual, CEOs never want to be in the position of having to explain a business case to their board without CFO sign-off on the numbers. It's not only necessary but prudent to get finance review, especially when an investment is so significant, in this case, a $2 million investment.

When we met with the CFO to review the proposed changes and investment needed, we told him that by implementing the recommended changes in human capital strategy, the investment would lead to an increase in shareholder value of $75 million. By the way, the CFO, CHRO, and the head of the business unit all had a significant number of stock options, so they all had significant "skin in the game." The CFO's reaction, as you might expect, was one of skepticism. He naturally asked, "How did you arrive at this figure?"

This was the test; answer this question credibly and convincingly and we'll get the CFO's buy-in. If not, we're dead!

We showed through the numbers, that by improving the human capital ROI for all of the units to the same level as the highest performing unit, it would result in an increase in EPS (earnings per share) of $.11. With about 36 million shares outstanding and a current trading multiple of 19, an $.11 increase in

EPS would lead to a $75 million increase in shareholder value. The CFO, had two reactions: 1. Walk me through the numbers again, and 2. Did the company have to commit the full $2 million investment immediately? We won! A really sharp GE-pedigreed CFO bought in to the methodology and all the numbers.

Thus, being able to show a credible impact on shareholder value will get even a sharp, skeptical CFO to support the business case for changes in human capital strategy.

THE MAGIC NUMBER

So what is the magic number that drives the value of the business? Well, it is not operating profit, because each company and division within companies define operating profit differently. There simply is no universally accepted definition of operating profit. Cross-industry or within industry comparisons are not possible. Also, nonoperating costs, such as interest and depreciation, are included in operating profit thus distorting the amount of profit a business is generating from its operations.

Neither is revenue the magic number. Not that revenue is irrelevant. While profits are a key driver of shareholder value for established organizations, revenue growth is also important. Campbell Soup is an example of a company where a lack of revenue growth hindered the growth in shareholder value. Under the reign of David Johnson, Campbell's had record growth in EPS for several consecutive quarters; however, the stock price increase was below what would normally be expected, given the increase in EPS. The reason? Lack of revenue growth! The EPS increase was being driven by aggressive expense management and the marketplace and stock analysts discounted the value of the EPS growth due to anemic growth in revenue.

The dot-com bubble was an example of revenue, not profits, driving shareholder value. At least until that bubble burst. At the time, companies were valued at several hundred times their projected earnings per share or several times their revenue because their revenue growth was so rapid. The thinking was that by being first to market in a given space, the growth would crowd-out the competition and ultimately lead to dramatic profits. While true in a few notable examples (i.e., Priceline, Amazon, and Ebay), these proved to be the exceptions. Nonetheless, revenue is a factor that drives shareholder value in both established and emerging companies.

However, in established companies revenue growth by itself will not drive shareholder value. Revenue increases will serve as an added EPS multiplier, provided that first and foremost, there is a growth in EPS. Those companies that have a steady increase in EPS coupled with a regular increase in revenue, especially organic revenue, tend to be recognized the most in the stock market.

While EPS is the ultimate number that Wall Street looks to each quarter, the measure of profit that drives EPS is EBITDA (pronounced EE-bid-dah) or earnings before interest, taxes, depreciation, and amortization. EBITDA is the most fundamental definition of profit for a business. This definition of profit normalizes for both the capital structure of the business and its tax status. Also, unlike operating profit, EBITDA is a universally understood concept among the financial community. Some financial experts think EBITDA is a better measure of a company's operating effectiveness because it ignores noncash charges altogether. A common misconception however, is that EBITDA represents cash earnings, it doesn't. EBITDA is a good metric to measure profitability, but not cash flow. EBITDA can also be used to compare companies against each other, and business units within the same company against each other and against industry averages.

As a measure of profit, EBITDA is used in a wide range of businesses. It offers a clearer reflection of operations by stripping out expenses that can obscure how the company is really performing. Interest, which is largely a function of management's choice of financing, is ignored. Taxes are left out because they can vary widely depending on acquisitions and losses in prior years and this variation can distort net income. Finally, EBITDA removes the arbitrary and subjective judgments that can go into calculating depreciation and amortization, such as useful lives, residual values, and various depreciation methods.

EBITDA is calculated by starting with net income after taxes as shown on the income statement. To this amount, add the interest and taxes, also found on the income statement. Then add depreciation and amortization, which can be found on the statement of cash flows. Voila, you have EBITDA. Some companies will report EBITDA in their annual report, thus making this task easy.

So, for the purpose of measuring the impact on shareholder value and making the business case, start with EBITDA, the magic number.

CALCULATING SHAREHOLDER VALUE

Before we provide the method to show how EBITDA ultimately drives shareholder value, here is the formula typically used on a day-to-day basis to calculate shareholder value for publicly-traded companies:

1. Earnings per share (EPS), times

2. Number of outstanding shares, times

3. Trading multiple (A valuation ratio of a company's current share price compared to its per-share earnings)

EPS is calculated by dividing net income after tax, by the number of outstanding shares. Net income after tax is included in the income statement. For example, Microsoft reported in its 2011 annual report that net income after taxes was $23.2 billion with fully diluted EPS of $2.69. This means there are approximately 8.6 billion shares outstanding ($23.2 billion divided by $2.69).

To calculate Microsoft's shareholder value during the 2011 fiscal year, we take its stock trading range, which was a low of $22.73 and a high of $29.46. Thus, based on an EPS of $2.69, the trading multiple ranged from a low of 8.4 to a high of 11.0 during the fiscal year. Therefore, Microsoft's shareholder value during the 2011 fiscal year ranged from a low of $194.3 billion to a high of $254.5 billion.

Fully diluted shares are the total number of shares that would be outstanding if all possible sources of conversion, such as convertible bonds and stock options, were exercised. Companies often release specific financial figures in terms of outstanding fully diluted shares (such as the company's profits reported on a fully diluted per share basis) to allow investors the ability to properly assess the company's financial situation.

For privately-held companies, the shorthand method for calculating shareholder value is EBITDA times a market multiple. A market multiple is the multiple of EBITDA that a buyer of the company, in an arms-length transaction, would pay to buy the company. A CEO or CFO can readily state the current market multiple for the company's industry. While there are several sophisticated accounting and financial methods to determine more precisely the value of privately-held companies, for day-to-day business planning purposes, it's common and acceptable to use the shorthand method described above (EBITDA x market multiple).

MEASURING THE IMPACT ON SHAREHOLDER VALUE

Measuring the impact on shareholder value is determined by the expected change in EBITDA resulting from the changes in human capital strategy. For example, in the financial services company described above, we compared the results of six homogeneous geographic units with varying levels of performance. Because we had a "naturally occurring experiment" we asked: What is the level of EBITDA (as a % of revenue) in the best performing unit? We then asked: What would be the impact on the dollar amount of EBITDA if all of the units had EBITDA at the same percentage of revenue as the highest performing unit? Because we had a homogeneous group, this was a credible method to project the amount of EBITDA potential, assuming all of the units performed at the same level (EBITDA as a percentage of revenue) as the highest performing unit.

Now that the potential EBITDA had been determined, this amount was reduced by interest, taxes, depreciation and amortization (ITDA) to calculate a revised net income after taxes. To simplify the calculation, there would be no change in these amounts (ITDA) from the original calculation of EBITDA. Alternatively, the amount of taxes would increase due to the higher level of taxable income, which could be reflected in the projected ITDA (line 2, below). The revised net income after taxes was then divided by the fully diluted outstanding shares to determine projected EPS. The difference between the current and projected EPS, multiplied by the fully diluted outstanding shares and the trading multiple was the impact on shareholder value.

Here is a worksheet to calculate the change in shareholder value for a publicly-traded company.

Shareholder Value For **Publicly-Traded Companies** Worksheet	Current	Projected
1. EBITDA (expressed in dollars and as a percentage of revenue)		
2. Interest, Taxes, Depreciation & Amortization (expressed in dollars)		
3. Net Income After Taxes (1-2)		
4. Fully Diluted Outstanding Shares		
5. Earnings Per Share (EPS) (3/4)		
6. Trading Multiple		
7. Shareholder Value (SV) (4 x 5 x 6)		
8. Change in Shareholder Value (SV Projected - SV Current)		

Here is a worksheet to calculate the impact on shareholder value for privately-held companies.

Shareholder Value For **Privately-Held Companies** Worksheet	Current	Projected
1. EBITDA (expressed in dollars)		
2. Market Multiple		
3. Shareholder Value (SV) (1 x 2)		
4. Change in Shareholder Value (SV Projected – SV Current)		

Again, it is important to keep in mind that if HR wants to get the CEO to invest in the changes in human capital strategy necessary to continuously improve business results and shareholder value, it is vital that HR make a "hard" business case for the recommended changes. Making the business case through shareholder value demonstrates a high level of business acumen which enhances HR credibility in the C-suite and boardroom. More important, it will focus the CEO's attention on the HR agenda since it speaks directly to his future wealth.

CHAPTER 6

READINESS ASSESSMENT

"Most of what is valuable is intangible, but most of what is measured is tangible."

–Herb Kelleher, Southwest Airlines

Before any organization can seriously commit to measuring and analyzing its investment in human capital (people and HR programs), it must first assess its current environment to determine the extent to which it can embrace and employ the concepts described in this book. Unless an organization is committed and equipped to accurately and promptly produce, and to precisely and thoroughly analyze the data and measures, any attempt to do so will quickly lead to failure.

There are several issues an organization needs to assess in order to determine the timing and the extent of its abilities to embrace the methods described herein. These issues include:

- Culture
- Alignment
- Data systems
- Resources
- Execution

At the end of this chapter is a questionnaire that can be used to determine the extent to which an organization is prepared to effectively implement human capital analytics.

CULTURE

As observed in Chapter Three, culture is quite an interesting and powerful phenomenon. It is the ubiquitous, invisible force that influences how organizations operate on a daily basis. Edgar Shein, Professor Emeritus of MIT Sloan School of Management, defines culture as "a pattern of basic assumptions invented, discovered or developed by a given group as it learns to cope with its problems of external adaptation and internal integration that has worked well enough to be considered valid and, therefore, to be taught to new members as the correct way to perceive, think and feel in relation to those problems". Whew, quite a mouthful. In short, culture is how groups interact and make decisions.

The cultural issue that plays a prominent role in how a company will embrace human capital analytics, is the extent to which there is top-down organizational commitment to business analytics. Is the analytics culture widespread throughout the organization? Are business decisions fact-based (data-driven) as opposed to opinion or gut-feeling based? Is there broad support for business analytics from the functional and operational areas of the business?

In the book *Crossing the Chasm*, Geoffrey A. Moore outlines what he calls the Technology Adoption Life Cycle (TALC). The concept describes at what point in a product life cycle potential customers will embrace a new product. Think of the TALC as a continuum with definable stages. There are parallels between human capital analytics and the Technology Adoption Life Cycle worth exploring.

The TALC includes five types of buyers:

- Innovators – Leaders who aggressively pursue breakthroughs and new ideas.

- Early Adopters – Visionaries that match emerging concepts and products to a strategic opportunity. They like fundamental breakthroughs and actively seek "state-of-the-art." They also like pilot projects because they "go where no man has gone before."

- Early Majority – Pragmatists are leaders who don't want to be pioneers. (Pioneers are people with arrows in their backs.) They avoid being early test sites as the "leading edge" is all too often the "bleeding edge." While visionaries like state-of-the-art, pragmatists like industry standard. They're comfortable being behind the curve.

- Late Majority – Conservatives that resist discontinuous innovations. They believe far more in tradition than in progress. They are well behind the curve and often only embrace a product or idea to avoid getting stung.

- Laggards – Skeptics that do everything in their power to block adoption of new products or ideas.

I've experienced the TALC phenomenon first hand. Earlier in my consulting career, I was the Flexible Compensation National Practice Leader for Foster Higgins during the "flex" hay days. I was on-point for most major flex consulting opportunities and often spoke on the topic at industry events. Our consultants around the country would call on me to meet with their clients and prospects about the merits of flex programs. What was so interesting in these meetings was how quickly we could determine where the company executives were on the TALC.

Invariably, each industry had their early adopters and these were the companies that would retain firms such as Foster Higgins to develop and implement a flex program. We also met with companies that were not going to implement a flex program until the industry leaders led the way. And then others that just had no interest in flex programs. What I found especially interesting was the HR subculture, as compared to the company's brand culture. For instance, the HR department of an industry leading technology firm were laggards as far as flexible benefit programs were concerned. This subculture flew in the face of a business that was viewed as leading edge with its technology products.

So, if your company or unit's culture is that of an Innovator or Early Adopter you're culturally ready to push the envelope and embrace these concepts and methods. It will be difficult however, to advance these concepts if your organization or HR function is an Early Majority (pragmatist), Late Majority (conservative), or a Laggard (skeptic). In those situations, watch closely what your industry leaders are doing with human capital analytics to determine how far you can advance these concepts in your own organization.

Another important cultural factor in determining your organization's readiness to use these tools is transparency. High levels of transparency in an organization's culture encourage an analytical orientation. Firms that are highly transparent will want employees and other constituencies to know about the data and analysis, particularly if they shed light on the business.

Having an analytical culture ensures that "how we do things around here" includes making decisions on the basis of data, facts, and rigorous analysis.

ALIGNMENT

Is there a consensus and understanding across the entire organization on the business strategy and the measures necessary to monitor alignment? As Kaplan and Norton observed in the *Balanced Scorecard*, in the ideal world, every person in the organization, from the boardroom to the backroom, should understand the strategy and how his or her individual actions support the "big picture."

To gain maximum benefit, the executive team should share its vision and strategy with the whole organization, and with key outside constituents. By communicating the strategy and by linking it to personal goals, there is a common understanding and commitment among all organizational participants. When everyone understands the business unit's long-term goals, as well as the strategy for achieving these goals, all organizational efforts and initiatives can be aligned to the needed transformational process.

Has HR worked with each line of business to establish specific, mutually understood expectations for targeted business outcomes? To illustrate, Campbell Soup Company also owns Pepperidge Farm and, at one time, Godiva Chocolates, yet each division had its own unique human capital issues influencing business performance. Hence, aside from a set of universal HR metrics on employee engagement, turnover, etc., each of the major business units had its own set of HR metrics targeted to its particular business strategy issues.

So, does HR have a thorough understanding of the business strategy and the human capital measures needed for each "client?" What does the "client" need to know to improve individual and organizational performance, and effectively implement the business strategy from a people perspective? The higher the stakeholder sits in the organization and the greater their span of influence/responsibility, the broader and more strategic will be the nature of their concerns.

In sum, the continuous challenge for HR will be: Can it demonstrate a linkage between human capital metrics and strategies, and business strategy priorities?

DATA AND SYSTEMS

The foundation of human capital metrics relies on data quality, reliability, integrity, and security.

W. Edwards Deming wrote: "In God we trust, all others must bring data." A statistician, professor, author, lecturer, consultant, and icon in the quality movement, Dr. Deming emphasized the importance of measuring and testing to predict typical results. If a phase consists of inputs + process + outputs, all three components are inspected to some extent. Problems with inputs are a major source of trouble, but the process using those inputs can also have problems. By inspecting the inputs and the process more, the outputs can be better predicted, and inspected less. Rather than use mass inspection of every output product, the output can be statistically sampled in a cause-effect relationship through the process.

Following Deming's advice, the input data needs to be carefully scrubbed to avoid the "garbage in" problem; the process phase calculates the measures relevant to the business and operating units; and the output produces insightful graphics and analysis that helps decide on the appropriate actions to drive improved business performance. Since this is a dynamic process, due to the fluid nature of the business and the markets in which the business operates, HR will need to be agile in readily modifying both the metrics and analysis to be relevant.

Here are some of the data and systems questions that HR must get satisfactory answers to in order to proceed with the concepts of this book:

1. HRIS – Is the core Human Resources Information System (HRIS) data complete and kept up to date? Are there best-of-breed HR support systems (talent, performance management, learning management, compensation and benefits, etc.) that need to be accessed for data?

2. HR service providers – Can necessary, accurate and up-to-date data be provided by relevant HR service providers?

3. Finance – Will HR have access to the financial system to calculate values and cross check HRIS data? According to the Hackett Benchmarking and Research reports, the typical company has twenty-nine different systems for each billion dollars of revenue.

4. Sales & Marketing – Will HR have access to the sales and marketing system to calculate values and cross check HRIS data?

5. Operations/Supply Chain – Will HR have access to the operations/supply chain system to calculate values and cross check HRIS data?

6. Information Technology – Will the IT function allocate and dedicate the resources necessary to extract, compile, and integrate the necessary data in a timely fashion?

Despite huge advances in enterprise resource planning (ERP) and other cross-enterprise integration technologies, many organizations still fail to adequately connect disparate data repositories. As a result, much of the available data remains disconnected, inconsistent, and inaccessible.

To address the data integration issue, companies have implemented single-purpose "data marts" and/or enterprise data warehouses (EDW) that cut across multiple functions and business units. Properly constructed, an EDW contains all the information that you might want to analyze. Vast and dynamic, EDWs are a more feasible avenue for analytics than working directly with transaction data. Unlike EDWs, data marts are departmental versions of data warehouses and are sometimes created independently of IT. Both of these data organization methods will help HR collect and analyze the data to help discern the root causes of human capital investment performance issues.

RESOURCES

By resources we mean people and money. From the money perspective, the issues are fairly straightforward. Has a budget been developed that identifies the magnitude and timing of the investments required? Are the financial resources available in the organization to execute the human capital metrics strategy? Is the company prepared, and does it have the will to invest in the technologies necessary to collect the data, build the algorithms and processes to calculate the values, and produce the metrics/outputs for the analysis to occur? Will the organization add or assign the technicians and analysts and accept the budget impact necessary to do the analytics work or will the work be outsourced?

As challenging as the financial issues may be, the people resources are more so. In his masterpiece *Good to Great*, Jim Collins wrote that the executives who ignited the transformation from good to great did not first figure out where to drive the bus and then get people to take it there. No, they *first* got the right people on the bus (and the wrong people off the bus) and *then* figured out where to drive it. So who are the right people that should be on the human capital metrics bus? The right people are superb analysts or technicians.

In their book *Analytics at Work* Tom Davenport and Jeanne Harris observed that they never saw an analytically oriented firm without plenty of analytically oriented people. Finding, developing, managing, and developing analysts-the people who make the day-to-day work of such organizations possible-is critical to a firm's success. Analysts are workers who use statistics, rigorous quantitative or qualitative analysis, and information modeling techniques to shape and make business decisions.

Davenport and Harris describe four types of analytical people: analytical champions, analytical professionals, analytical semiprofessionals, and analytical amateurs:

- Analytical champions are executive decision makers who depend heavily on data analyses to make business decisions and who lead major analytical initiatives. Analytical champions have both strong business acumen and an appreciation of analytical techniques.

- Analytical professionals create advanced analytical applications by developing statistical models and algorithms to be used by others in the organization. Professionals typically employ advanced techniques such as trend analysis, classification algorithms, predictive modeling, statistical modeling, and optimization and simulation, as well as a variety of data,

Web, and text mining techniques. The best professional analysts are not only technical and quantitative, but also skilled at explaining analytical problems and results in clear and nontechnical language.

- Analytical semiprofessionals apply the models and algorithms developed by analytical professionals on behalf of the rest of the business. Their primary role is to apply analytics to business problems for routine or specialized decision making. They are experts in data creation, collection, interpretation, and use. They perform complex queries and run models on data, link the analyses and insights to business results, and prepare business reports based on these analyses.

- Analytical amateurs are employees whose primary job is not analytical work, but who need some understanding of analytics to do their jobs successfully. Amateurs are knowledgeable consumers of analytics who can apply analytical insights to their work. They also summarize and report data to others in their organization.

Quantitative skills are the core requirement for any type of analyst. But effective analysts need to be proficient not only with data, but also with people. Here is a list of the competencies required of analysts:

o *Quantitative and technical skills* are the foundation. Analytical people must know how to use the software tools associated with their type of analytical work, whether it is to build algorithmic models, define decision-making rules, conduct "what-if" analyses, or interpret a business dashboard.

o *Business knowledge and design skills* enable analysts to be more than simple backroom statisticians. They must be familiar with the business disciplines and processes to which analytics are being applied.

o *Relationship and consulting skills* enable analysts to work effectively with their business counterparts to conceive, specify, pilot, and implement analytical applications. Relationship skills-advising, negotiating, and managing expectations are vital to the success of all analytical projects. Furthermore, an analyst needs to communicate the results of analytical work; either within the business to share best practices and to emphasize the value of analytical projects; or outside the business, to shape working relationships with customers and suppliers, or to explain the role of analytics in meeting regulatory requirements.

> o *Coaching and staff development skills* are essential to an analytical organization, particularly when a company has a large or fast growing pool of analysts, or when its analytical talent is spread across business units and locations.

Analysts are an interesting and challenging group to manage successfully. From my management experience, analysts and technicians are similar to actuaries and health and welfare consultants. As a region manager for Foster Higgins I had management responsibility for a group of pension actuaries, and health and welfare actuaries and consultants. Actuaries, H&W consultants, and analysts are motivated by interesting and challenging work that allows them to use their highly specialized skills. This is provided by variety in their work and a sense of personal progress. Analysts also want to do important work that makes a meaningful contribution. The models and applications they build must matter to the business. Analysts want to feel supported and valued by their organizations, but they also want autonomy at work—the freedom and flexibility to decide how their jobs are done. Analysts like to be surrounded by other smart and capable colleagues. We called them pods of actuaries. Companies that can offer analysts the chance to work with other smart analysts and business people have little trouble attracting analytical talent. As we recruited actuaries and consultants from other firms, one of the first questions they asked was who else was on the team. Analytical people also seek a strong culture of trust. Positive relationships with their immediate supervisors are also particularly important to analysts.

Lyle Spencer, Jr. and Signe Spencer have also identified a list of 12 competencies for analysts or technicians in their book *Competence at Work*. (Analysts and technicians fit into the same job category.) While the competencies are similar in nature to those described by Davenport and Harris, the Spencers prioritize the competencies and provide a different perspective. Of these competencies those with the greatest weight are:

- Achievement orientation. The single most frequent distinguishing characteristic of superior technical contributors. Their main focus is on measuring performance or outcomes against a standard of excellence and on improving outcomes of performance in some way.

- Impact and influence. One of the most frequently mentioned distinguishers of superior performance. Technicians primarily use direct persuasion, supported by data, concrete examples or demonstrations, facts and figures, and graphic presentations to make their case. They are concerned about the impact of their ideas and about establishing professional credibility.

- Conceptual and analytical thinking. These two competencies combined would be the most frequent distinguisher of technical stars. Analysts need both logical, deductive analytical thinking and conceptual thinking. Analytical thinking is demonstrated most often as breaking tasks into component parts in a rational systematic manner. Analytical thinking also appears as anticipating and planning for obstacles or seeing the implications or consequences of situations. A more inductive conceptual thinking is equally important: seeing connections and patterns that others don't see: condensing large amounts of information in a useful manner; identifying key actions to take to resolve a murky situation; identifying underlying problems. Conceptual thinking also involves putting together information from different areas.

- Initiative. Initiative appears as tenacity or perseverance in sticking with a difficult problem until it is completed. Initiative is also a matter of taking advantage of present opportunities or addressing present problems before being required to do so. Initiative is demonstrated in going beyond the required or expected effort to get the job done.

The other 8 competencies described in the Spencers' book include: Self-confidence, interpersonal understanding, concern for order and quality, information seeking, teamwork and cooperation, expertise and customer service orientation.

The Spencers and Davenport and Harris provide a compelling picture of the types of people companies require to effectively execute a human capital analytics strategy and work plan.

EXECUTION

Using Collins' bus metaphor, a key question is *"who is driving the human capital analytics bus?"* More important, *"who should be driving the bus?"* In other words, who should and can, most effectively, do the HR or human capital analytics? Should it be the HR, finance, or the IT function, or a combination of all three? While HR are the subject matter experts, finance regularly measures business results and analyzes the factors driving the results, while IT typically owns the data, and the software and tools necessary to conduct the analytic process.

In our view, HR needs to take the lead on human capital analytics because the people side of the business has not typically been a strength of either finance or IT. Also, HR is best equipped to develop and recommend the right human capital strategy recommendations to continuously improve business results. And by leading the analytic process, it furthers HR's goal to be an integral part of, and have significant influence, in the C-suite. While HR should lead the process, both finance and IT must be engaged partners in the process.

Just do it!

I'm reminded of Nike's tagline–"Just Do It" and the admonition–"Perfect is the enemy of good." The point is--begin the journey, somewhere. While we argue that an organization should begin by measuring the human capital ROI, productivity, and liquidity (for all the reasons explained in Chapters Two, Three, and Four) you should begin the journey wherever your organization is best equipped to do so. Even if you decide to start with traditional HR metrics, we believe you will quickly find your way to the benefits of measuring the human capital ROI, productivity, and liquidity, and embracing the analytic process described in Chapter Four. The Chinese philosopher Lao-tzu is credited with the saying "A journey of a thousand miles begins with a single step." So, take that single step and while it may not be perfect, you will be one step closer to having the data needed to make compelling, data-driven, fact-based human capital strategy recommendations that will drive future business performance.

As you plan that single step forward, pilot test an initial approach. My client Campbell Soup used pilots to great effect. In fact, the CHRO believed that if his direct reports weren't always doing pilots on some aspect of their service portfolio, they weren't doing their job. As you would expect, some of the pilots failed while others succeeded and were subsequently successfully leveraged throughout the Campbell Soup operating divisions.

As you pilot an initial approach, begin to develop an implementation plan including time line, budget and resources needed for a full-scale program execution. The knowledge gained by conducting the pilots will provide the insights to craft an effective implementation plan. This is part of the business case argument. The pilot will help you figure out the most effective approach to a full-scale launch and begin to gain consensus on the completion of the program.

Finally, to maintain momentum, it will be necessary to communicate and continuously sell the initiative, throughout the organization, for ongoing executive commitment.

In closing this chapter, let's look to the stars. We've often heard the observation that the stars are aligned to undertake some significant initiative within an organization. It is then that the organization will commit the money, time, and people to effectively engage the initiative.

To review, in order for there to be a commitment to human capital analytics, the stars that need to be aligned are:

- Culture – Culture is a fact-based, data-driven environment that drives business decisions with a strong bias towards transparency.

- Alignment – There is a consensus on the organization's goals and the business strategies including HR's role in achieving the goals.

- Data – Data systems have been or will be implemented that will provide the data to effectively analyze the factors driving organization performance.

- Resources – The organization is staffed properly with analysts to effectively analyze the data and tease out the factors driving performance and the most effective solutions. Financial resources have been committed for the necessary data systems and analyst staffing.

- Execution – HR will own and drive the human capital analytics bus, and is prepared to test pilot different approaches to identify the most effective path forward while simultaneously developing a comprehensive implementation plan.

When an organization can answer yes to each of the above five items, it can then say with confidence that the stars are aligned to embrace human capital analytics.

HUMAN CAPITAL ANALYTICS
Readiness Assessment

To assess your organization's readiness to effectively implement human capital analytics, complete the questionnaire below, analyze your responses, make your conclusions, and then describe a path forward. Each question should be assessed at the company, business unit, and HR department level.

Culture

Which of the following categories best describes your company, business units, and HR Department?

    1. Innovator/Early Adopter

    2. Early Majority

    3. Late Majority/Laggards

To what extent are business decisions data-driven, fact-based vs. opinion or gut feel? (Scale 1 to 10)

To what extent is there a top-down commitment to business analytics? (Scale 1 to 10)

To what extent does transparency exist within your organization? (Scale 1 to 10)

Alignment

To what extent is there a consensus across the organization on its business goals and strategies? (Scale 1 to 10)

Data

To what extent is the data in the HRIS and HR support systems kept up-to-date? (Scale 1 to 10)

Can HR service providers provide up-to-date data promptly and regularly? (Scale 1 to 10)

To what extent can the following systems provide up-to-date data?

    # Financial

    # Sales & Marketing

    # Operations/Supply Chain

Data (contiued)

To what extent will IT dedicate resources to extract, compile, and integrate the data in a timely fashion?

Has your organization established and maintained an enterprise data warehouse (EDW)?

Has the HR department established a data mart for HR data?

Resources

Has a budget been developed that identifies the required investment?

Are financial resources available to execute the human capital metrics strategy?

Will the necessary technicians and analysts be hired or assigned to do the analytics work?

Execution

Is there senior executive sponsorship for human capital analytics?

Are pilot projects an accepted method to test ideas?

Is someone prepared to continuously communicate and sell the initiative throughout the organization?

CHAPTER 7

FINAL OBSERVATIONS

"If you always think as you've always thought,
You'll always do what you've always done.
If you always do what you've always done,
You'll always get what you've always got.
If you always get what you've always got,
You'll always think as you've always thought."
—Author Unknown

In this closing chapter we attempt to put into context the notion of human capital analytics and its place in the broad context of business intelligence. We also offer some perspectives on a couple of the contemporary issues in the human capital analytics field.

As we have discussed earlier, in the twenty-first century, maximizing a company's human capital is a key competitive factor for success. If human resources leadership is to be effective and add value in support of this effort, they must operate as business leaders. This means that all aspects of the human capital strategy must be aligned with and in furtherance of the organization's business strategy. The language of the C-suite and the boardroom are numbers and strategies. Analytics applied to human capital issues are essential in providing data that will allow leadership to manage this valuable asset more effectively.

Unfortunately, most companies' measurement systems typically deliver a blizzard of nearly meaningless data that quantifies practically everything in sight, no matter how unimportant; that is devoid of any particular rhyme or reason; that is so voluminous as to be unusable; that is delivered so late as to be virtually useless; and that then languishes in printouts and briefing books, without being put to any significant purpose. In short, as Michael Hammer observed in his book *The Agenda*, measurement is a mess.

To counter Hammer's observations, human capital analytics needs to be a process, not a one-time event. Like other business processes such as Total Quality Management (TQM) or Six Sigma, human capital analytics requires a continuous improvement mindset. By standardizing an approach to a very important and challenging business problem, we reduce errors and better understand the factors that drive success. This ultimately reduces costs and increases effectiveness.

Turning mountains of data into useful concepts is an iterative process of looping back and forth, developing ideas and testing them against the data, revising the ideas, building a framework, seeing it break under the weight of evidence, and rebuilding it again. The process is repeated over and over again, until everything hangs together in a coherent framework of concepts.

All measures and metrics need to be put into the appropriate framework. Never view any measure in isolation. A measurement framework lets you see the relationships and trade-offs between measures.

Measurement of human capital doesn't much matter if it is not part of a process. Like any metric, it must be used to stimulate change and drive people to take action. Ultimately, the human capital analyst needs to do the following with data to transform it into a performance management process that informs decision making:

- Trend it.
- Benchmark it.
- Set goals against it.
- Dashboard it. Having a dashboard with drill-down capabilities is a great way to emphasize the governance associated with metrics.
- Compare it to plan or budget. Evaluation data is great and can be tapped to review the past and forecast the future.

THE FUTURE OF HUMAN CAPITAL ANALYTICS

Other distinguished people in the human capital analytics field have offered their observations on the future of human capital analytics and the need to focus on effectiveness. In *The New HR Analytics* Ed Gubman, Founder and principal of Strategic Talent Solutions, and former Executive Editor of *People & Strategy*, offered the following observation on the future of human capital analytics. "Our field has been pursuing better human capital metrics for a long time now, but despite some real creativity, we are hampered by lack of agreement on the big-outcome measures. We have trouble getting metrics to capture mind share and popular usage because we have nothing comparable to finance's ROI, net income, and the like. And, without accepted outcome measures, deep-dive HR analytics leads us further into the trees without knowing where the forest is. Until we do these things, we will have sequoia-size measurement aspirations and sapling-size realities."

Ed Lawler, Alec Levensen, and John Boudreau of the Center for Effective Organizations (CEO) published a paper (CEO Publication G 04-8 (460)) titled "HR Metrics and Analytics Uses and Impacts." Though brief, the paper's Executive Summary concludes that if HR aspires to be a genuine strategic partner, it must collect and use effective data. The summary reads as follows:

Whether and how the HR Function in corporations uses metrics and analytics is studied. The results indicate that HR functions often collect data on their efficiency. However, they often do not collect data on the business impacts of their programs and practices. This is a crucial point because the results show that those HR organizations that collect effectiveness data are more likely to be strategic partners. This finding suggests that if HR wants to play a strategic role in organizations it needs to develop its ability to measure how human capital decisions affect the business and how business decisions affect human capital.

Used along with the necessary resources to transform data into insights, workforce analytics enable HR professionals to be more engaged in the formulation of corporate strategy. The result is better fact-based decision-making capability that is aligned with the long term business imperatives of their organizations.

In sum, Spitzer, Gubman, Lawler, et al. offer a compelling argument for a business context for human capital analytics and the need to focus on effectiveness.

THE BUSINESS ANALYTICS CONTEXT

Human capital analytics is late to the field of business analytics. While there are many definitions of analytics, the definition included in "Analytics: The Widening Divide," a paper by IBM Global Business Services and MIT Sloan Management Review is perhaps the best –"Analytics: The use of data and related insights developed through applied analytics disciplines (for example, statistical, contextual, quantitative, predictive, cognitive and other models) to drive fact-based planning, decisions, execution, management and learning. Analytics can be descriptive, predictive or prescriptive."

This paper was based on insights gathered from more than 4,500 managers and executives as part of the 2011 New Intelligent Enterprise Global Executive Study and Research Project, which identifies three key competencies that enable organizations to build competitive advantage using analytics. The initial study in 2010 identified three progressive levels of analytical sophistication: Aspirational, Experienced, and Transformed

Analytical Sophistication			
	Aspirational	**Experienced**	**Transformed**
Percentage of total respondents	32%	45%	24%
Analytical use	Basic user	Moderate user	Strong and sophisticated user
Reliance on analytics	To guide decision making in financial management and supply chain management	To guide future strategies, and increasing reliance on analytics to guide activities in marketing and operations	To guide decision making in day-to-day operations and future strategies across the organizations
Information foundation	Few standards are in place; structured, siloed data supports targeted activities	Enterprise data integration efforts are underway	Enterprise data creates integrated view of the business with a growing focus on unstructured data
Analytical tools	Primarily uses spreadsheets	Expanding portfolio of analytics tools	Comprehensive portfolio of tools to support advanced analytics modeling
Analytical skills	Ad hoc analysis is done at point of need; has difficulty hiring analytics talent	Analysts work in line-of-business units with growing focus on cross-training and hiring skills externally	Many are combining line-of-business units with centralized units that provide advanced skills and governance
Culture	Managers are focused on executing day-to-day activities	Open to new ideas but lacks top-line leadership and champions to support changes	Strong top-line mandate to use analytics supports a culture open to new ideas and champions who shepherd methodology and skills

Overall, organizations that used analytics for competitive advantage were 2.2 times more likely to substantially outperform their industry peers. Transformed organizations in that group were 3.4 times more likely to do so.

Propelled by the digital transformation of entire industries and the globalization of business operations, leading organizations continuously re-evaluate and re-define the strategic decisions that underpin their success. Almost three out of four Transformed organizations use analytics to guide their future strategies. By using analytics across the enterprise to monitor, detect, and anticipate events, organizations are learning to avoid unnecessary risk.

The study found that in order to achieve analytics sophistication, organizations typically master three competencies: 1. Information management, 2. Analytical skills and tools, and 3. Data-oriented culture. Companies with a strong information foundation are able to tackle business objectives critical to the future of the entire enterprise. Their robust data foundation makes it possible to capture, combine and use information from many sources, and disseminate it so that individuals throughout the organization, and at virtually every level, have access to it.

Organizations that deploy new skills and tools for analytics can typically answer much harder questions than their competitors. Competency in *analytical skills and tools* can be achieved through internal development and cross training or external hiring and outsourcing in areas such as advanced mathematical modeling, simulation, and visualization.

In a data-oriented culture, behaviors, practices, and beliefs are consistent with the principle that business decisions at every level are based on analysis of data. Leaders within the organizations that have mastered this competency set an expectation that decisions must be arrived at analytically and can explain how analytics is needed to achieve their long-term vision. Organizations with this culture are likely to excel at innovation and strategies that differentiate them from their peers. In these data-driven cultures, expectations are high. Before "giving the green light" to a new service offering or operational approach, for example, leaders ask for the analytics to support it.

While a significant investment in money, time, and people is necessary to achieve the Transformed status, the question should not be how much money do you spend on data and analytics; but how much value are you getting from them?

Centers of Excellence

As organizations explore the field of human capital analytics, an issue that will surface is whether to establish a Human Capital Analytics Center of Excellence. Not for the faint of heart, Centers of Excellence require a significant investment of people, money, and time. We define a Center of Excellence (CoE) as a dedicated team with the capability to extract and interpret data and communicate its implications to stakeholders within the business. In short, the CoE delivers fact-based observations and ideas to influence human capital strategy that will drive business results.

Getting meaningful business information out of HR systems is a challenge for many HR organizations. A greater challenge still is the need for HR to provide deeper insights about an organization's human capital. For example Gartner estimates that 70% to 80% of all corporate business intelligence projects fail to deliver the expected value. Why is it so hard to turn human capital data into business insights? And why is it that HR seems so far behind finance and marketing in its ability to answer critical business questions? One reason is that compared to other business functions, HR measurement is in its infancy.

To transform human capital data into meaningful insights that can drive strategic decisions requires a specific set of skills that cannot be built overnight. There also needs to be a dedicated group whose primary focus is human capital analytics.

Success Factors identified nine items for creating a successful human capital analytics centers of excellence.

1. Appoint an analytics CoE champion to build support. A successful CoE requires sponsorship by a senior level HR executive who will evangelize the benefits of a human capital analytics function and clearly articulate how the CoE model will best deliver value.

2. Review existing processes in a new light. A key step at this stage is to clean up historical data, instead of just implementing rigorous data standards on a go-forward basis. A tedious and time consuming task, cleaning up historical data is necessary to ensure credibility of findings. This review should also be performed to evaluate the merits of any existing report on human capital.

3. Find the right talent to build the human capital analytics CoE team. A successful CoE requires a mix of analytical, consultative, and communication skills. One key point is to have the right people on the team at the right time. It is important not to "over hire" and take on someone whose skills will be little used during the initial development of the CoE. The CoE needs to be able to do the basics first, and do them well in order to be credible.

4. Choose the right structure. Until the CoE has demonstrated proven results, resources may need to be borrowed, shared or distributed. This approach may prove challenging from a resource allocation standpoint. There can be benefits to starting out with a decentralized analytics delivery model. Building a human capital analytics function provides excellent opportunities for learning and development, and the chance to help HR become more data driven is appealing to many HR professionals. The opportunity to develop analytics expertise and become a stronger strategic partner with business executives will help attract employees to the analytics team.

5. Have a clear vision and shout about it. CoEs benefit from a clearly defined vision statement that is circulated among key business partners.

6. Choose quick win projects that showcase CoE value. Instead of trying to "boil the ocean," quick wins will more readily help establish the credibility of the CoE. These projects should be limited in scope and have a clear relationship to the bottom-line performance of the organization.

7. Collect data that can be trusted and used. Nothing risks credibility more than basing an analysis on flawed data. Getting the data right is a lot of work, but the payoff is substantial.

8. Use the right tools for the job. The benefit of using robust tools adds significant value by:

    a. Reducing the amount of time spent on low-value data activities

    b. Increasing the capacity for innovation by reducing the time needed to revise analyses

    c. Avoiding the battle of the spreadsheets requiring reconciliation from disparate sources of data

9. Establish a process and communicate your brand. Developing consistent processes, and a recognizable look and feel for the CoE's output, will help to establish credibility and company-wide familiarity. Coupled with valuable analysis, the CoE brand will generate confidence in the product and the capabilities of the team.

We'll close this section with an observation from McKinsey in the March 2011 edition of *McKinsey Quarterly*: "New tools and methods for analyzing data enable HR to define the link between 'people practices' and performance more effectively…the upshot: if you and your head of HR haven't recently discussed ideas for using data to generate a talent strategy that's more closely linked to business results, it's time to start."

COMMENTS ON A FEW CONTEMPORARY ISSUES ON HUMAN CAPITAL ANALYTICS

About Lagging Indicators

As noted in my biography, I am a member of the Society of Human Resources Task Force on Measures and Metrics. SHRM, as an American National Standards Institute (ANSI) designated Standards Developing Organization, is sponsoring the development of American National Standards in the area of HR Measures and Metrics. There is a wonderful group of folks participating in this initiative from around the world in academia, industry, consulting and technology communities. The goal of our invigorating discourse is to seek consensus on the metrics we believe the investor community, among others, would find of value.

In the course of these discussions there has been a healthy debate on the value of leading and lagging indicators. Detractors of lagging indicators argue that they are of little value and that the task force should focus on leading indicators. While acknowledging the value of leading indicators, detractors of lagging indicators are missing the main value of lagging indicators; they are outcome measures. As such, lagging indicators define the precise outcome of prior actions. Having precise outcomes helps organizations compare the actual outcomes versus the expectations of human capital strategy actions that were implemented. Did we achieve what we expected when we approved action "x" or "y"? What did we learn from this outcome about the actions that were taken? How does this outcome influence our future actions?

This debate on leading vs. lagging indicators is taking place in numerous forums, not just the SHRM Task Force. For instance, it can be seen on LinkedIn and other social networking groups.

As mentioned previously, I was the Flexible Compensation National Practice leader for Foster Higgins. As part of a feasibility study to help clients determine whether to implement a flex program, we would do 3-to-5-year cost projections to show the financial impact of the programs. After flex program implementation it was common practice to reconcile actual costs (outcome, lagging indicator) with the initial financial projections. The questions that followed were, as you would expect, did we meet the financial projections? If not, why not? Given the actual cost (lagging indicator), what actions can we take to achieve new cost targets? Hence, it was a dynamic process; no different than any other aspect of a vibrant business.

So, while leading indicators will be a valuable element of the metrics landscape, lagging indicators should continue to play a necessary and important role in the human capital metrics domain.

Predictive Analytics

Related to the issue of leading versus lagging indicators is the discussion taking place on predictive analytics. Predictive analytics relates what we know currently to what we want to know about the future. Whereas descriptive analytics reveals current data patterns, predictive analytics gives meaning to those patterns for the future. With practice, one can look at historical data and foretell, to some degree, the likelihood of a future occurrence.

Predictive analytics expresses the future in terms of probabilities. It helps management make decisions that minimize risks and increase ROI. No analytic application can predict the future with absolute certainty; but, when properly applied it will reduce variability.

While an intriguing concept, it carries with it its own set of issues. Amit Mohindra, Director of Primary Research for the Institute for Corporate Productivity (i4cp), penned a piece on the topic in *Talent Management* magazine entitled:"The Road to Analytics." Amit observed that there are significant pitfalls with predictive analytics: The problem is that relevant statistical models, such as logistic regression or data mining approaches, are complex. They are hard to explain and the results need to be qualified with so many statements the audience soon loses interest and confidence. Further, the outputs from predictive analytics are denominated in probabilities, odds and likelihoods, numbers the average person isn't comfortable interpreting, Last but not least, because results are probabilistic in nature, there's no guarantee a prediction will come true. When it doesn't, no one will remember the prediction was qualified; woe to the talent manager unfortunate enough to make two faulty predictions in a row.

While predictive human capital analytics holds potential promise to help companies make better human capital strategy decisions, companies are well advised to proceed with extreme caution.

Total Cost of Workforce: An incomplete definition of costs resulting in misinformation and false results

In the ongoing attempt to capture the total amount of money a company spends on human capital, a relatively new concept has emerged: Total Cost of Workforce (TCOW). While this is a forward thinking initiative, it tends to overlook costs. Consequently, TCOW can't be trusted as a measure to calculate any economic value metric such as productivity or ROI.

There are several definitions of TCOW. The Human Capital Management Institute defines TCOW as the total costs of all salaries, wages, and direct and indirect cash or equity compensation for all employees. TCOW includes:

- all costs for contingent, temporary, or contract workers whenever the organization primarily directs the work of such labor. For example, offshore employees who work in a separate legal entity that is 50% or greater controlled by the organization should be included in the total cost of workforce.

- all company provided or paid employee benefits, perks, and rewards. Such costs also include all company retirement related costs for both current and former employees.

- all enterprise training costs provided to employees and or contingent labor.

- all recruiting costs not already included incurred as workforce acquisition costs.

- all employee relations, severance, and legal settlements paid to current and former employees or contingent labor.

Human Capital Source defines TCOW as compensation and benefits, and HR service costs.

Human Concepts defines TCOW as the sum of all workforce related costs, including all compensation, benefits, and other employee costs. Total cost of employees includes all employee related costs for the organization for a given period of time. The workforce is defined as employees plus contingent (contract and temporary) workers.

The problem with these definitions is that they are incomplete. As defined by these organizations, TCOW makes it impossible to make informed business decisions relevant to human capital because TCOW ignores outsourcing costs. Kaplan and Norton observed the problem of outsourcing costs in *The Balanced Scorecard*. The example they used was revenue per employee and the same would be true for any measure where any of the above TCOW definitions are used as the denominator. Kaplan and Norton said: any time a ratio is used to measure an objective; managers have two ways of achieving targets. The first, and usually preferred way is to increase the numerator–in this case increasing revenues without increasing the denominator (the number of employees). The second, and usually less preferred method is to decrease the denominator–in this case, downsizing the organization, which might yield short-term benefits but risks sacrificing long-term capabilities. Another way of increasing the revenue-per-employee ratio through denominator decreases is to outsource functions. This enables the organization to support the same level of revenue but with fewer internal employees.

By ignoring outsourcing costs, the denominator, as Kaplan and Norton observed, can be easily manipulated to artificially inflate any metric influenced by TCOW. I saw this firsthand with a client trying to reconcile the difference in performance between two divisions. The TCOW in division A was lower than division B, yet the margin in division A was also lower than in division B. The CFO expected that division A would have a higher margin because of a lower TCOW. Upon deeper investigation, the CFO discovered that division A outsourced technology support services, thus driving down the TCOW. However, division A's overall expense load, as a percentage of revenue, was higher than division B, thus resulting in a lower margin.

If the client had used the definition of human capital costs explained in Chapter Two, this problem of misinformation would have been avoided altogether. Moreover, the CHRO and CFO would have quickly discovered that outsourcing costs were having an adverse impact on margin.

In conclusion, as currently defined, companies should avoid the use of Total Cost of Workforce as a human capital metric or an element in a human capital metric formula because TCOW doesn't represent a company's entire amount spent on human capital. Consequently, any result using this method will be misleading, thus working at cross purposes with HR's goal of increasing its influence in the C-suite and boardroom.

MOVING FORWARD

I hope this book has given you a specific and constructive path forward to most effectively use the financial resources your company devotes to human capital. The more that HR can craft, implement, and manage human capital strategies that drive improved productivity the greater the chances for prosperity for your company and society overall.

It seems we are reaching a tipping point. The field of human capital analytics is in its infancy but is rapidly evolving and will continue to do so. HR departments are hiring analysts, technology companies are developing increasingly robust tools to gather and analyze data, and HR consultants are dedicating significant resources to help clients collect and analyze data to identify the precise human capital strategies that will drive improved business performance. All of these actions bode well for future business performance and the role that HR will play in driving that success.

As we move forward, it is vital that companies communicate how they are effectively using human capital analytics to drive HR strategy and business performance. In future editions of this book or subsequent books we will focus on case studies that demonstrate the successful connection between human capital analytics, the resulting HR strategies, and the enhanced business performance. So, please share with me your human capital analytic experiences, and challenge our methods and perspectives.

In response to the quote at the beginning of this chapter, if you want to change what you have always done, you can't think as you've always thought. Using the approaches laid out in this book will change the way you've always done human capital analytics, resulting in new and effective ways of setting human capital strategy that will have profoundly positive effects on your business results.

APPENDIX A

SAMPLE DATA DEFINITIONS

PROFESSIONAL SERVICES

VIENNA HUMAN CAPITAL INDEX™

HUMAN CAPITAL DATA-SET DEFINITIONS AND EXPLANATION OF CALCULATIONS

CONTENTS

- **Introduction**
- **Data set definitions**
  - Revenue
  - Human capital costs
    - Employee costs
    - HC costs – in support of employees
    - HC costs – in lieu of employees
    - Expenses not considered HCC
  - Financial Capital Costs
- **Vienna Human Capital Index Calculations**
  - Productivity
  - Human Capital ROI
  - Profit Sensitivity

INTRODUCTION

- The Vienna Human Capital Index measures the productivity, return on investment, and liquidity of Professional Services' entire investment in human capital. This data is compiled into the Vienna Human Capital Index for the fiscal years ending in 20xx and 20yy.

- To calculate productivity, return on investment and liquidity, Professional Services provided information from Professional Services financial reports and the Professional Services general ledger. Except for shareholder equity, all of the information used in calculating the values is derived from Professional Services general ledger, income statement and balance sheet.

- The purpose of this document is to record what data was used in the calculations, how the calculations were done, and the key assumptions used in the calculations.

- The sources of the data are:

  - Excel spreadsheets from Professional Services finance: "Professional Services profit and loss 12 months ended December 31, 20xx and 20yy." These spreadsheets give line by line data on revenue and direct operating expenses.

  - Research on the relationship of revenue to shareholder equity of selected professional service firms. These are all publicly-traded companies.

DATA-SET DEFINITIONS

REVENUE

1. Revenue consists of revenue for the US operating regions (Central, East, NY Metro and West) excluding National/Other.

2. There is no investment income identified in the total revenue amount.

3. Client reimbursable expenses reduced revenue to determine a total revenue amount that was used in all the calculations.

HUMAN CAPITAL COSTS

There are three categories of human capital costs:

- Employee costs
- HC costs - In support of employees
- HC costs - In lieu of employees

The 20xx Expense data is a combination of data from two financial systems as shown on the Excel spreadsheets. The expense category descriptions below are based on the current financial system.

1. **Employee costs:** *Compensation, benefits, and payroll taxes*
   - All of these items are posted as reported, except as noted in bold italics
   - Salaries are not sensitive to revenue or profit. The general category is "Salaries & Wages" and includes exempt salaries, non-exempt salaries, holiday pay, vacation pay, bereavement pay, allocated salary changes, sick pay, and accrued vacation benefit. In addition, severance (51901) is included in this category.
   - Incentive compensation, as reported and includes Bonus-Project, commissions, 51770 (annual bonus based on company performance for all employees), and a couple of other miscellaneous items. *51770 is the only element of incentive compensation directly sensitive to the profitability of Professional Services.* Account 51770 was allocated among the business units based on a percentage of salaries. *A more appropriate allocation method would be actual amounts paid by business unit.*

- Employee benefits, as reported and includes other benefits ($3,826,791), pension cost, hosp & medical, LTD, 401(k) match, FICA, unemployment tax, life insurance, supp 401(k) Employee Inc/L, retiree medical, retirement plan, Workers' Compensation. Pension costs, Supp 401(k) Employee Inc/L and retirement plan expense were allocated among the business units on a salary proportional basis.

- Overtime, as reported

2. **HC Costs - In support of employees:** *Costs that are incurred primarily to support the employee. By and large, these costs would not be incurred except for the presence of employees. In accounting terms these costs would be called variable costs.*

- Employee relocation

- Purchased services: Cafeteria subsidy (52511)

- Travel and Entertainment (Management conferences (52540), auto expense (52339, 52815, 52820,52830)

- Personnel related costs, all line items

- Forms and supplies: Office supplies (52120) and facilities supplies and service (52190) are considered human capital costs. All other line items in this category are considered "cost of doing business" expenses.

- Occupancy (all accounts other than janitorial service, warehouse rent, and security service)

- Telecom Services (all accounts except for: Video/audio conferencing, telephone-leased lines, external website fees, and EDP line costs)

- General expense item I/C HIPAA expense

3. **HC Costs - In lieu of employees:** *Amounts paid to vendors for services that otherwise would be provided by an employee. This category of human capital expense is also referred to as substitution costs.*

- All of the amounts are as reported.

- Temporary services (689660.512990): All line items, except for Severance, which is considered an employee cost.

- Purchased Services: No items. The only question is outside services (52546). This line itemizes "Consists of debit card expenses for HSA line of business, certain printing expenses, surveys, research, food service. This is a catchall account where a lot of misc. fees are dumped."

- Professional and Consulting: All of the charges for line items management consulting fee, outside other admin. fees, and outside human resources; and 20% of outside accounting service (52530). The balance (80%) is audit fees.

- Occupancy: Janitorial service (52238) and security service (54140) are the only line items in the category.

- Other general expenses: The following line items: Intra-group expense tran (53100.226), I/C human resources C/O (53100.835), I/C A/P processing (53100.209), I/C call center expense (53100.830), I/C management fee (53100.640). All of these expenses were allocated among the business units on a revenue proportional basis. Is this appropriate or is there a more appropriate basis on which these expenses should be allocated among the business units?

- Expense Allocation: The total expense allocation for US operating regions for 20xx was $24.5 million. 50% of this amount was charged as a human capital cost. This category of expense is for "corporate allocations into Professional Services from groups outside of Professional Services. It includes IT, HR, finance, audit, legal and office services."

Direct Operating Expenses NOT Considered Human Capital Costs

These expenses are incurred by the business irrespective of the presence of employees. These fall into the general categories of costs of doing business and/or sales and marketing expenses. These expenses are all in the "general expense" category.

- Equipment expense-All line items
- Purchased services-All of the line items in this category, except for cafeteria subsidy (52511)

- Travel and entertainment-All of the line items in this category, except for management conferences, auto expense – mileage, tolls and parking, gas and other

- Marketing and Customer Relations-All line items

- Forms and Supplies-All line items, except for office supplies, computer and equipment supplies and facilities supplies and service

- Legal services-All line items. Should any of these costs be considered human capital costs, in lieu of employees?

- Postage

- Delivery charges

- Occupancy-Warehouse rent (54112) only

- Telecom Services-The following line items are considered business expenses: Video/Audio conferencing, telephone-leased lines, client internet expense, external website fees, and EDP line costs. The remaining line items are considered "in support of" employees.

- Other General Expenses-The following line items are considered business expenses: Collection agency fees, insurance and surety, I/CGHRS TPA fee, sales tax, other taxes & licenses, tax penalties, charitable contributions, default liability reserve, I/C Network G&A expense, I/C microfiche/ microfile, I/C help desk allocation, I/C information systems.

FINANCIAL CAPITAL COSTS

There are four items included in financial capital costs:

1. Interest

2. Depreciation

3. Amortization

4. Cost of Equity

1. Interest Expense – *These amounts are allocated on a revenue proportional basis. The entire Interest Expense was allocated among the operating regions. No portion of this amount was allocated to National/Other. Is this the most appropriate method to allocate interest expense?*

2. Depreciation – These amounts are as reported.

3. Capital Leases – This is not applicable.

4. Acquisition Amortization – *These amounts are allocated on a revenue proportional basis. The entire acquisition amortization amount was allocated among the operating regions. No portion of this amount was allocated to National/Other. Is this the most appropriate method to allocate Amortization?*

5. Cost of Equity – This amount is 12% of estimated Shareholders Equity, allocated on a revenue proportional basis. As described earlier, Vienna researched the relationship of shareholder equity to revenue for several publicly-traded similar organizations. The average relationship was 53%. We used this percentage as a proxy for the unavailable actual amount of Professional Services shareholder equity. *Is allocation on a revenue proportional basis the most appropriate method to allocate shareholder equity?*

VIENNA HUMAN CAPITAL INDEX CALCULATIONS

This section describes how the Index and strategic metrics were calculated. The Vienna Human Capital Index calculates productivity, human capital return on investment, and profit sensitivity.

- Productivity: To calculate productivity we used revenue, human capital costs and financial capital costs both actual and planned for the year. *To calculate "Productivity: Plan" we added to revenue the difference between Actual and Plan PTP (Pre-Tax Profit).*

- Human Capital ROI: To calculate human capital return on investment we use profit (EBITDA) less all financial capital costs, both actual and planned for the year. The balance is divided by human capital costs. To calculate HC ROI Plan, we used PTP Plan for the year and added to that amount interest, depreciation and amortization. This gave us "Plan EBITDA." EBITDA is used to calculate the return on human capital. *Over and above the cost of capital, what is a minimum return Professional Services expects to achieve on its investments on a pre-tax basis?*

- Profit Sensitivity: To calculate profit sensitivity we used the actual amounts paid. We also assumed the amounts paid are the target amounts.

While we were provided actual amounts for fiscal years 20xx and 20yy, the financial plans for those years were not provided. *We were provided with information that 20xx results were 6% below PTP Plan, and 20yy results were 7% above PTP Plan for the fiscal year.* Based on these results we built EBITDA and productivity plan amounts to compare against actual results. *This is necessary to calculate an overall Index value.*

In summary, to perform the calculations we used:

- Revenue, as reported and adjusted by Vienna HCA as described above
- Human capital costs, as described above
- Financial capital costs, as described above
- Shareholders equity, as described above
- PTP (pre-tax profit), as reported
- Profit target (PTP) for the fiscal year ending in 20xx was $35,518,000 (est.)
- Profit target (PTP) for the fiscal year ending in 20yy was $27,045,000 (est.)
- Profit (EBITDA), as described above

HUMAN CAPITAL STRATEGY MAP

DIAGRAM

The Vienna Human Capital Index™ measures the financial performance of a company's investment in human capital. The diagrams on the next three pages illustrate the analytic, cascading process that identifies the precise human capital strategy actions needed to continuously improve Vienna Index™ results and business performance.

VIENNA INDEX DIAGRAM

This diagram illustrates the process to dissect and analyze the Vienna Index results. This process will identify the financial factors driving the results. Each element of the formulas is dissected and can be examined as a percentage of revenue and percentage of change over time.

HR METRICS DIAGRAM

This diagram illustrates the process of discerning which HR metrics are driving the Vienna Index results.

These measures are examples of typical HR metrics. They are not intended to be all inclusive and may vary from division to division, within an organization. The HR metrics are organized into the four major elements of the Vienna Human Capital Strategy Model: Talent, Rewards, Culture, and HR Services.

HUMAN CAPITAL STRATEGY REVIEW DIAGRAM

This diagram illustrates the issues to be probed to identify the precise human capital strategies to improve business performance. These issues are not intended to be all inclusive and may vary from division to division, within an organization. The goal is to gain consensus among the stakeholders on the human capital strategy actions that will drive future business results.

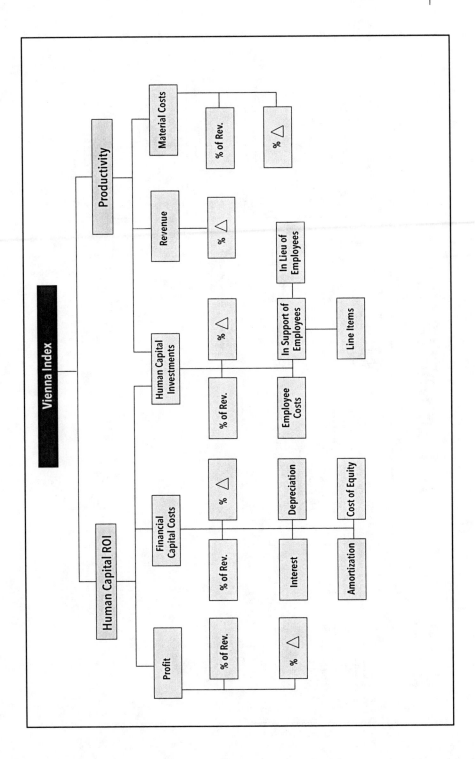

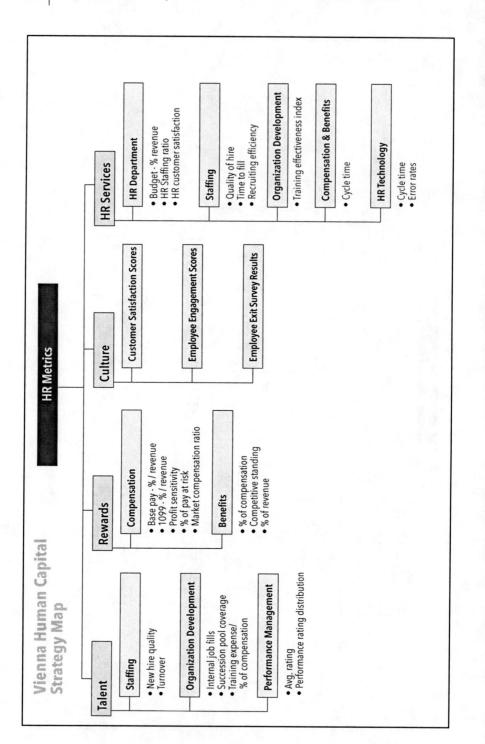

Vienna Human Capital Strategy Map

HR Metrics

Talent

Staffing
- New hire quality
- Turnover

Organization Development
- Internal job fills
- Succession pool coverage
- Training expense/ % of compensation

Performance Management
- Avg. rating
- Performance rating distribution

Rewards

Compensation
- Base pay - % / revenue
- 1099 - % / revenue
- Profit sensitivity
- % of pay at risk
- Market compensation ratio

Benefits
- % of compensation
- Competitive standing
- % of revenue

Culture

Customer Satisfaction Scores

Employee Engagement Scores

Employee Exit Survey Results

HR Services

HR Department
- Budget - % revenue
- HR Staffing ratio
- HR customer satisfaction

Staffing
- Quality of hire
- Time to fill
- Recruiting efficiency

Organization Development
- Training effectiveness index

Compensation & Benefits
- Cycle time

HR Technology
- Cycle time
- Error rates

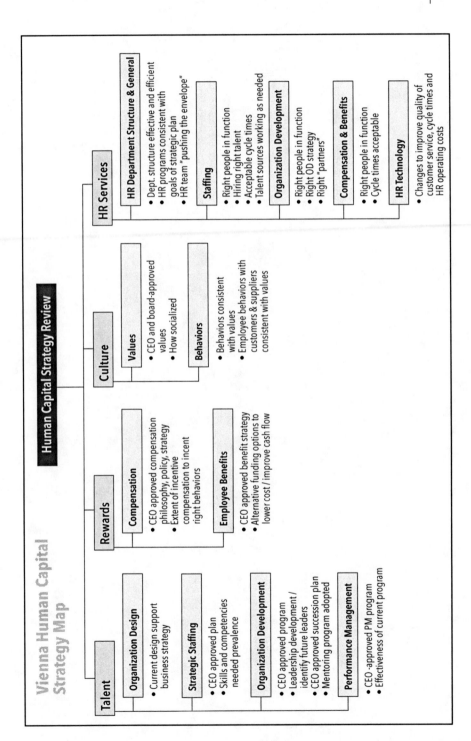

Vienna Human Capital Strategy Map

Human Capital Strategy Review

Talent

Organization Design
- Current design support business strategy

Strategic Staffing
- CEO approved plan
- Skills and competencies needed prevalence

Organization Development
- CEO approved program
- Leadership development / identify future leaders
- CEO approved succession plan
- Mentoring program adopted

Performance Management
- CEO -approved PM program
- Effectiveness of current program

Rewards

Compensation
- CEO approved compensation philosophy, policy, strategy
- Extent of incentive compensation to incent right behaviors

Employee Benefits
- CEO approved benefit strategy
- Alternative funding options to lower cost / improve cash flow

Culture

Values
- CEO and board-approved values
- How socialized

Behaviors
- Behaviors consistent with values
- Employee behaviors with customers & suppliers consistent with values

HR Services

HR Department Structure & General
- Dept. structure effective and efficient
- HR programs consistent with goals of strategic plan
- HR team "pushing the envelope"

Staffing
- Right people in function
- Hiring right talent
- Acceptable cycle times
- Talent sources working as needed

Organization Development
- Right people in function
- Right OD strategy
- Right "partners"

Compensation & Benefits
- Right people in function
- Cycle times acceptable

HR Technology
- Changes to improve quality of customer service, cycle times and HR operating costs

APPENDIX C

HUMAN CAPITAL STRATEGY MAP

WORKSHEET

LEVEL I ANALYSIS – HCROI, PRODUCTIVITY AND PROFIT SENSITIVITY

HUMAN CAPITAL ROI:

Overall results:

Improving?	YES	NO
On plan?	YES	NO

Results consistent across divisions or wide dispersion?

Is the ROI at target level?	YES	NO

Which business units are underperforming?

EBITDA:		
Improving ($ and % of revenue)?	YES	NO
On plan?	YES	NO

Results consistent across divisions or wide dispersion?

Which business units are underperforming?

Financial Capital Costs:		
Improving as a % of revenue?	YES	NO
On plan?	YES	NO

Results consistent across divisions or wide dispersion?

Which business units are problematic?

Human Capital Costs:		
On plan?	YES	NO
Improving as a % of revenue?	YES	NO

Results consistent across divisions or wide dispersion?

Which business units are problematic?

Productivity:

Overall results:		
Improving?	YES	NO
On plan?	YES	NO

Results consistent across divisions or wide dispersion?

Which business units are underperforming?

Revenue:		
Increasing?	YES	NO
On plan?	YES	NO

Results consistent across divisions or wide dispersion?

Which business units are underperforming?

Material Costs (MC):		
On plan?	YES	NO
Improving as a % of revenue?	YES	NO

Results consistent across divisions or wide dispersion?

Which business units are underperforming?

Profit Sensitivity:

Results consistent across divisions or wide dispersion?

EBITDA plan:

What is the overall EBITDA plan as a % of revenue?

Is EBITDA plan, as a % of revenue, consistent across divisions or wide dispersion?

Is EBITDA plan increasing as a % of revenue?	YES	NO

Profit-driven Incentive Compensation (PdIC):

What is the overall PdIC plan as a % of EBITDA plan?

Is the PdIC % of EBITDA consistent across divisions or wide dispersion?

Is the PdIC ratio at a target level?	YES	NO
Is the PdIC level increasing as a % of EBITDA plan?	YES	NO
LEVEL II ANALYSIS - HUMAN CAPITAL COSTS (HCC)		
Overall results:		
Are HCC decreasing as a % of Revenue?	YES	NO
Are HCC consistent across divisions as a % of Revenue?	YES	NO

Which business units are problematic?

Employee costs:		
Are employee costs decreasing as a % of Revenue?	YES	NO
Are the results consistent across divisions?	YES	NO

Which business units are problematic?

Are there specific line items increasing at a disproportionate rate to revenue?	YES	NO
Costs in support of employees:		
Are employee support costs declining as a % of Revenue?	YES	NO
Are the results consistent across divisions?	YES	NO

Which business units are problematic?

Are there specific line items increasing at a disproportionate rate to revenue?	YES	NO
Costs in lieu of employees:		
Are substitution costs decreasing as a % of Revenue?	YES	NO
Are the results consistent across divisions?	YES	NO

Which business units are problematic?

Are there specific line items increasing at a disproportionate rate to revenue?	YES	NO

NARRATIVE ON LEVELS I AND II RESULTS

HR METRICS

The HR measures below are for illustrative purposes only. A company's specific set of HR measures must be selected and monitored against expectations to identify areas of potential problems. A measurement scale also needs to be selected to assess performance.

TALENT

New hire quality
Development quality/internal job fills
Successor pool coverage
Turnover
Voluntary
HIPO voluntary
Retention rate
Average performance appraisal rating
Training expense per FTE

REWARDS

Profit sensitivity
Bonus eligibility rate
Market compensation ratio
Healthcare costs as a % of compensation
Benefit costs as a % of compensation
Compensation and benefits as a % of revenue
Total compensation expense per FTE
Unscheduled absence rate
Unscheduled absence days per employee

CULTURE

Employee engagement score
Customer satisfaction scores
Employee exit survey results

HR SERVICES

HR Department

HR operating budget as a % of revenue
HR staffing ratio
Hiring manager satisfaction
HR customer satisfaction

Staffing/Recruiting

Quality of hire
New hire failure factor
Recruiting Cost Ratio (RCR)
Time to fill vacancy rate
Referral rate
Recruitment source ratio
Offer acceptance rate

Organization Development

Development program participation rate
Average performance appraisal rating
Training hours per FTE
Training effectiveness index
Successor pool coverage

Compensation and Benefits

Direct comp expense per employee
Bonus eligibility rate
Avg. % of pay at risk

HR Technology

HR Technology expense rate
HR T transaction error rate

NARRATIVE ON HR METRICS

HUMAN CAPITAL STRATEGY REVIEW

The following questions are designed to help a company assess the effectiveness of the human capital strategy. The questions are not intended to be all inclusive, but illustrative of the questions that need to be asked to determine if the existing human capital strategy needs to be changed in some manner to improve the Vienna Human Capital Index and HR metrics results, and overall business performance.

TALENT

Organization Design

Does the current organization design support our business strategy?

Strategic Staffing

Has a strategic staffing plan been defined and accepted by the CEO?

Does your team have the skills and competencies needed to achieve the vision and goals in the strategic plan? What about the departments that you interact with?

People Development

Is there an employee professional development program that meets the business needs and that will help the company achieve its vision?

Is there a leadership development program that identifies future leaders and their respective development needs?

Is there a succession plan in place that will ensure a smooth transition in leadership?

Do employees need any formal or informal mentoring programs to enhance performance?

Performance Review and Management

Do you have any observations about the performance management program's ability to meet the company's goals and vision?

REWARDS

Compensation Design and Funding

Is there a defined compensation philosophy and strategy?

Does the compensation system (pay and bonuses) enable us to attract and retain the people we need to achieve the strategic plan, goals, and vision?

To what extent is incentive compensation necessary to motivate the right behaviors? Should the compensation program be used to recognize outstanding employees?

Employee Benefits Design and Funding
Is there a written employee benefit strategy?
What are the strengths and weaknesses of the employee benefits program? Are there features about the program that should be changed align it with the strategic goals?
Are there methods of funding the benefit programs that will lower costs and improve cash flow?

CULTURE
Values and Behaviors
How would you define the company culture? Does this culture foster employee commitment to the company, its vision, and strategic goals?
Do employees behave in ways consistent with or contrary to the values stated in the strategic plan?
Are employees behaviors with customers and suppliers consistent with the values defined in the strategic plan?

HR SERVICES
HR Department Structure and General
Is the HR Department organization structure designed to effectively and efficiently respond to the needs of its constituents?
Are there any HR programs that are inconsistent with the vision and goals of the new strategic plan?
Are there HR services that should be changed to better serve the needs of the business?
Is our HR team "pushing the envelope" by suggesting and pilot testing new ideas?
Staffing and Recruiting
Are the cycle times acceptable?
Are our talent sources working as needed?
Are we hiring the right talent?
Do we have the right people in this function?
Organization Development
Do we have the right OD strategy?
Do we have the right people in this function?
Do we have the right "partners"?
Compensation and Benefits
Do we have the right people in this function?
Are the cycle times acceptable?
HR Technology
What changes in technology will result in improved cycle times and lower HR operating costs?

NARRATIVE ON HUMAN CAPITAL STRATEGY AND PRIORITIES

SUMMARY OF HUMAN CAPITAL STRATEGY RECOMMENDATIONS
AND FINANCIAL IMPLICATIONS

ABOUT THE AUTHOR

Frank J. DiBernardino

Frank, a 35-year veteran of the Human Resources consulting world, is the founder and Managing Principal of Vienna Human Capital Advisors LLC. He has consulted with organizations in manufacturing, health care, pharmaceuticals, transportation, financial services, petroleum, technology, and academia.

Before launching Vienna HCA, Frank was a Principal at Mercer and a Founding Principal of Foster Higgins. He began his consulting career with Johnson & Higgins. His background includes strategic planning, client relationship management, consulting practice leadership, labor negotiations, underwriting, staff development, and line management.

As a thought leader in the evolving field of human capital analytics, Frank developed and patented a breakthrough human capital analytics tool that precisely measures the financial performance of an organization's human capital investment (people and programs).

Frank has also developed a comprehensive, cohesive, and cascading HR strategic planning process to convert human capital financial results into specific strategy actions that will continuously improve business results.

Frank serves on the SHRM Measures and Metrics Task Force which is developing American National Standards for Human Resources.

Frank has had articles published in Directors & Boards magazine, *Directors & Boards* e-Briefing, and *People & Strategy* (HRPS peer review journal) on measuring the economic value of companies' investment in human capital.

Over Frank's career his clients included: Amdahl, Boeing Helicopter, Bristol-Myers Squibb, Buck Consultants, Campbell Soup, Duke University, First Union (now Wells Fargo), IBM, Johns Hopkins University, Memorial Sloan-Kettering Cancer Center, Norfolk Southern, NYU, *Reader's Digest*, Robert Wood Johnson University Hospital, Sunoco, Tesoro Petroleum, and Tulane University.

He served as the national practice leader in both Health & Welfare and Flexible Compensation practices and developed sophisticated strategic planning tools to enable clients to reliably measure the financial impact of benefit and compensation alternatives.

A creative and resourceful thinker, Frank pioneered the concept of Personal Financial Security as the overarching theme for a 10-year public policy strategic plan adopted by The American Benefits Council.

Frank has served on the Board of Directors of the American Benefits Council, the Employers Council on Flexible Compensation, and the Editorial Advisory Board of *Benefits Quarterly*. In addition, Frank is a founder and past President of PEBA, the Penjerdel Employee Benefits and Compensation Association.

He has been awarded the professional designations of Certified Employee Benefit Specialist (CEBS) and Chartered Life Underwriter (CLU).

Frank has lectured frequently on human resource issues to organizations such as:

- The Conference Board
- American Benefits Council
- American Management Association (AMA)
- Society for Human Resource Management (SHRM)
- World at Work
- College and University Personnel Association (CUPA)
- National Association of College and University Business Officers (NACUBO)
- Employers Council on Flexible Compensation (ECFC)
- Financial Executives International (FEI)
- Philadelphia Human Resource Planning Society (PHRPS)

INDEX

CPSIA information can be obtained at www.ICGtesting.com
Printed in the USA
LVOW080955291012

304872LV00001B/2/P